Learning to Build Apps
Take On Silicon Valley Using the Tools It Created

MCS Mahone

Learning to Build Apps
Take On Silicon Valley Using the Tools It Created

MCS Mahone

True Anomaly LLC
8351 Ronda Dr
Canton, MI 48187

Disclaimer

While considerable effort has been made to ensure the accuracy of the information herein, this book is intended for teaching beginner programmers and may contain simplifications or other technical inaccuracies. If you feel any of the content is incorrect and would like to suggest a revision, or if you find typos or other errors, you may submit them to contact@trueanomaly.com. Pease include the book title, page number, and error details in your email.

Neither the publisher nor the author assume any liability for errors, omissions, or damages resulting from the use of the information contained in this book. Code snippets contained in this book are provided with no warranty expressed or implied. Use of information, code and links provided in this text is at your own risk.

Legal Issues

No part of this book may be reproduced, stored or transmitted in any way, without the written permission of the publisher, except for brief quotations.

Some of the products and services mentioned in this book may be claimed as trademarks. When the publisher was aware of a trademark claim on the designation, the designation was printed with an initial capital letter.

Open source code mentioned in this book may be subject to license and other intellectual property restrictions.

Table of Contents

Preface

Not long after my college graduation, I grew tired of my family asking why I wasn't rich like Mark Zuckerberg. I felt I had unrealized potential, but my dreams lay scattered and broken like plastic cups after a fraternity party. Until one morning—with a new dash of ambition—I decided to teach myself web programming. I opened an Internet browser, typed in the address of a popular online bookstore, and started buying.

Fast forward five years, to the moment of my epiphany—as I sat amongst dozens of programming textbooks, pages of online help files, piles of notebooks filled with sloppy writing—when I realized nearly all of the knowledge I had just acquired had staled. In the five years it took to teach myself Linux server administration, Apache, SQL, Object Oriented PHP5, JavaScript, HTML, CSS, and AJAX, the world had changed. The mobile web had taken off: HTML had become HTML5, CSS had become CSS3, the static web had become responsive, JavaScript had moved to the server, and background updates had become real-time. JavaScript had acquired an array of enterprise level development and build tools with indecipherable names. It was then—that horrible moment, after five years of study—when I realized I had gotten nowhere. I considered myself a web developer, as I had put some respectable sites online, but the website was dead, killed by the web app and the mobile app. Despite all of my hard work, web development blogs and publications had once again become a confusing mess of names and acronyms about which I knew nothing: responsive grids, NPM, Node.js, Firebase, WebSockets, Service Workers, Promises, Generators, ECMAScript6, and many others. Switching to native app programming for iPhone and Android required a whole different education, but the learning curve for web apps did not seem much less intimidating. After five years of studying, it was as if I hadn't even started. I sat back and wondered, how did this happen? How had I managed to waste so much of my time? What was I going to do now?

Purpose

I can't promise that something similar won't happen to you. Without doubt technology will change during your study as well, but I can help you get up to speed quickly to minimize the amount of wasted time and effort. When I look back on those initial years I ask myself, "why was it so hard?" I know the answer: I spent a lot of time figuring out what to learn, almost as much time as I spent learning it.

This book provides a roadmap of the confusing maze of acronyms, giving you guidance on what needs to be learned and what you can skip. Self-taught learning requires knowing what books to buy, where to find the community online, and where to find documentation and resources. Often I purchased books only to discover they were not relevant. I also invested hundreds of hours learning languages only to watch technology shift so rapidly that my hard earned knowledge had become nearly worthless. This book cannot eliminate these challenges, but by charting a rapid path forward it will allow you to learn efficiently so that when technology changes, you won't find yourself heavily invested in the wrong topics.

This book will help speed your journey to the bleeding edge of web / native application development by providing a map and information to get past the obstacles I faced as a self-taught learner. Many minor roadblocks are invisible to the more educated computer programmers out there (who write the majority of programming textbooks), and any concepts that I struggled to grasp are addressed in this book. In addition, this book provides top-level overviews of core Internet technologies that—while very brief— should contain just enough information for you to continue on your path.

The goals of this book are as follows:

1. Show how all technologies on which mobile applications depend fit together
2. Provide sufficient background knowledge on the aspects of the technology stack relevant to mobile development
3. Define a specific, albeit biased, path from zero to mobile developer, while also pointing out alternative routes
4. Serve as a sufficient prerequisite to learning mobile development

This book will not teach you how to program or build mobile apps. Instead, it is a guidebook and a map. Web and mobile development are built on top of a massive technology stack. In Chapter 1 we present a roadmap that shows how each of the topics fit into this stack. We also highlight what this book will teach, and what it will not teach. This will allow you to visualize how the topics in the web development section of the bookstore fit into the larger picture. You won't know everything about everything, but you will know to which part of the stack a particular acronym pertains and whether it is relevant to your journey.

Chapters 2-5 will focus on the background knowledge that will help you along as a mobile developer. These chapters are neither extensive nor exhaustive but contain enough to allow you to learn to program more easily.

In Chapter 6 we present a smaller, more detailed roadmap that illuminates a very specific section of the larger map. This detailed map contains a path to learning programming and mobile application development using languages of the web. There are other ways to build mobile apps, using other web technologies or native development. The book simply aims to enlighten so that you may choose the most appropriate path for your goals.

Finally, Chapter 7 will discuss tools and techniques that will allow you to hit the ground running when you begin to learn programming. The appendix contains some random topics that I struggled to grasp during my study and may help you overcome these roadblocks.

Who This Book Is For

Perhaps you are a skilled trade professional who recognizes the need to learn programming in this rapidly changing world. Perhaps you are a high school student trying to find a quick way to riches. Or perhaps you can relate to my story: you are a college grad who realized a bit too late that a computer science degree may have been a better choice! As different as these life stories are, they are united by one common thread: we may not have a passion for computers, apps or programming, but we see learning mobile development as a means to an end, whether that end is simply survival, or fortune. Current lack of passion does not mean that a talent for programming cannot be awakened, however, and that is where this book comes in. Diverse life experiences are an asset, not a liability, as you are better able to see opportunities for apps and technology that the computer science geniuses cannot.

Prerequisites

I assume you are a brand new, aspiring web / mobile developer, perhaps with an idea for the next big thing. I assume you are highly motivated and anxious to get started, but I do not assume that you have any programming experience, nor do I expect that you have the slightest idea where to begin. Quite the opposite, in fact, I assume you have felt absolutely overwhelmed by the apparent chaos in the titles of computer programming books. However, I do assume you have used a computer extensively, and feel comfortable with web browsers, a smartphone, files and folders and one or two operating systems (Windows or Mac OS X).

Companion Website

Almost all of the content in this book is — or will be — discussed in video form on the MCS Mahone YouTube channel https://www.youtube.com/channel/UC3-MYnHYaYIqZejdiQRorJA/.

Errata may be found at https://trueanomaly.com, and code contained in the book at the GitHub page at https://github.com/trueanomaly/trueanomaly.github.io.

Contact Us

If you have questions about the material, reach out to me using @mcsmahone on Facebook, Twitter, or Instagram.

If errors or technical inaccuracies are found herein, please contact us at contact@trueanomaly.com. Please include in the message the page number and quotation of the error.

Please address all other inquires to:

True Anomaly LLC
8351 Ronda Dr
Canton, MI 48187

Ready? Let's Go!

Before you begin, note that I do not expect that you will master each concept from this book alone. This book merely intends to introduce the necessary information, with the expectation that greater understanding will come with further study of the map provided. If some of the topics seem too esoteric, do not give up! Keep moving forward confidently. Even after finishing the book, many concepts will not make sense until you continue down the path. Keep this book handy as a reference and a guide.

I never did build the next big thing. My work never went big time, but I did enjoy learning and continue to enjoy the challenge of programming, and if I can help you make your dream a reality than it will all be worth it. I hope you wake up each morning excited to learn. I hope you look out at the world and see nothing but opportunity for you and your new idea, and maybe one day I will have the privilege of using the app you build with the help of this book.

CHAPTER 1
What Is An App?

This chapter will define and discuss two types of mobile applications: **native apps**, and **web apps**. We will make the distinction between web and native clear very soon, but let's begin with the most basic question in application development, "what is an application, really?"

To answer this, we need to talk briefly about desktop computer programs. Desktop programs allow us to peek under the hood more easily than mobile apps, so don't fear when they are mentioned, we will return to our focus on mobile development shortly.

An application (a.k.a. a program) is an **executable** or interpretable* file of code. However, since nearly all major programs are composed of multiple files, I think it is easier to think of an application as a folder of files. Surprisingly, that's it! A program is just a folder of files regardless of whether we are talking about a mobile app, a web app or an app that runs on a desktop computer. The files in the application folder can contain code or data. The code files contain functions, which are like recipes or instructions to complete a certain task. The data files might be configuration information in a special format, or images or other graphics. There is also a special file known as an executable file. This file contains code that works like the ringleader of the circus, gathering together all of the other files when needed to put on the show. The executable file is in a format (binary digits, more on those later) that can be immediately understood and therefore "run" by a computer.

---

*For now it is sufficient to think of compiled code as a file of zeros and ones, and interpreted code as human readable code that will be turned into zeros and ones by an interpreter program. For a more robust definition and details on the difference between compiled and interpreted programming languages see a computer science textbook or search the web.

Opening this file will run the program and in that program the code will likely reference other files within the application folder. Files that contain binary data are often called **binaries**, and they are not human readable (they just look like a bunch of zeros and ones).

Figure 1-1 A .app file on an Apple computer is actually a folder containing resource files such as icon graphics and images, and an executable file. When you click on the application icon, or double click on a program shortcut on Windows, you are running the executable file in the corresponding application folder.

Figure 1.1 shows how to view this folder on an Apple computer. We can view the contents by right clicking on a program and clicking "Show Package Contents".

To get a better concept of what else is in this mysterious folder, open up a program on your computer. You see all those icons in the toolbar, like the printer, or the paintbrush or the save disk, and many others? Those are all graphic or image files that are stored in this folder, and opening the executable file (a.k.a. running the program) instructed your computer to grab those graphics files and display them in a certain place within the application window. Every graphic displayed, the code for every action or behavior (like a click to open a menu or dialog), and everything this program shows and does, is defined by a file in the application folder.

Now you may be wondering how this relates to mobile apps. A mobile app is a folder of files too, and tapping the icon on the smartphone home screen "runs" the executable file in this folder. In fact, programming for smartphones is not fundamentally different than programming for desktops. Both smartphones and desktop computers are computers, with processors and hard drives and operating systems. Each operating system has a programming language that is considered "native", meaning that it requires no additional environment to run programs. **Objective-C** and **Swift** are the programming languages used on both Mac Apps that run on the Mac OS X operating system, and iPhone and iPad apps that run on the iOS operating system (although Swift is the more modern language and is now the standard). The programming languages **Java** and **Kotlin** can be used to write native applications for Android, and can also be used to write applications on other operating systems if the user has the proper "environment" installed. For now, just realize that smartphones are mini computers, with different but related operating systems to their larger cousins, and each operating system has a programming language that is considered native. Programs that are written in the language native to an operating system are called native applications. Figure 1-2 shows two common operating systems and their native languages.

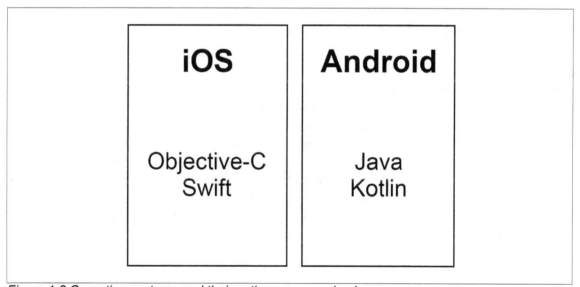

Figure 1-2 Operating systems and their native programming languages.

As an aside, you may have noticed that some applications for desktop or laptop computers can simply be downloaded and copied into your Applications folder (or Program Files on Windows) and then run, while others need to run an installer program first. Why the difference? Applications that require an installer likely want to add or modify system wide libraries. An example is a word processor. This software has font definition files (files that tell a computer how to display a certain font on the screen). Rather than put these files in the application folder (where only one program would be know how to find them), the installer program moves the font definitions to a font library folder on your operating system. Technically, if the software maker wanted their customers to do the work they could leave all the file transfer operations to the end user, but since software makers want to cater to non-computer savvy individuals, they usually take the extra step and write an installer program that puts everything in the proper place automatically. In addition, the installer program may check your computer's compatibility and modify configuration files (that the executable may reference for settings) as appropriate. In contrast, applications that simply can be downloaded and run are completely self-contained, meaning all the files they require are contained in their application folder, and they do not need to modify or add files to your operating system.

Web Applications

In addition to native applications, every smartphone or desktop with a web browser can run web applications. You are probably very familiar with websites; web apps are not very different. As the web became more and more ubiquitous, people wanted websites to behave more like native applications, and thanks to improvements in a programming language called **JavaScript**, they now do. Web applications differ from native applications in where they are stored and the programming language used to write them, as well as the environment in which they run. The difference between native apps and web apps is shown in Figure 1-3. As you can see, web browsers act as an intermediary between the application and the computer much like an interpreter helps two people who speak different languages communicate.

4

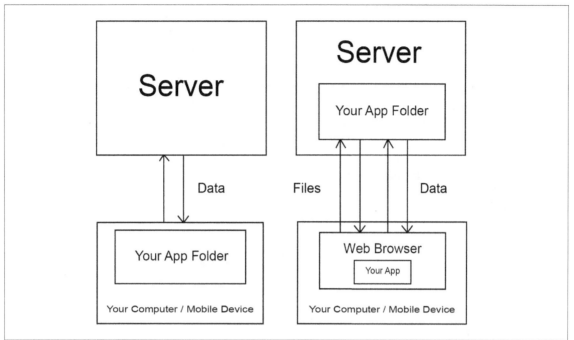

Figure 1-3 Native apps run directly on the OS. Web apps are stored on a remote server and run through a web browser.

Web applications are nothing more than a folder of files too, but in web applications, this folder is not stored on the end user's hard drive but rather on a server, that **hosts** the file (hosting just means "makes available via the Internet"). In web programming there is technically no executable file but all web programs have one file, typically called index.html, that is opened by a web browser and interpreted on the fly. Unlike the executable files mentioned previously, index.html is written in human readable HTML and either contains JavaScript code or links to other files containing JavaScript code.

The web browser accesses the other files inside the folder when it deems necessary. Index.html contains the relative file locations of any additional files (images, CSS, JavaScript), so these can be accessed with additional requests. Your web browser makes those additional requests in the background and completely unbeknownst to the end user. An example application folder for a web application is shown on the left side of Figure 1-4.

When you open a web browser such as Firefox or Chrome, and type in example.com into the address bar, your browser sends a request across the Internet for the index page (a.k.a. file) from example.com's web server. This index file contains links that tell your browser where to find the images on the page, such as the logo. Once your browser receives the index file from the server, it sees that it needs those image files as well, and so it sends additional requests to the server for them. All these requests and responses happen in milliseconds to seconds, so the end user never even knows that they are happening. Once the browser has all the data it needs, it builds and displays the page according to the instructions in the code. An example of a web browser rendering a web page is shown on the right side of Figure 1-4.

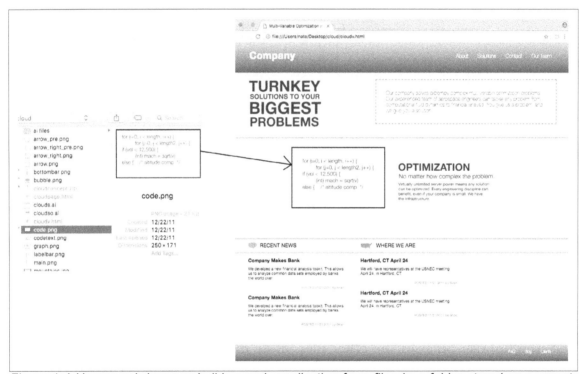

Figure 1-4 How a web browser builds a web application from files in a folder stored on a remote server is just like how a native app grabs files off of the local hard drive to display them in the app. This shows the image file named code.png displayed in a web browser.

The chief advantage of web applications is that they don't have to be installed locally on a computer, they are accessible from every computer, regardless of operating system, from anywhere in the world, on both desktops and smartphones. This makes the ability to write web applications an extremely powerful skill.

Let's Review

So far we have learned that an application is a folder full of files with a special file that can be run, or executed in programmer speak. There are two types of applications, native and web. Both are folders of files, but there are two major differences between native platform coding and web programming: the programming language used, and how the end user gets the program on their computer. With native applications (whether for desktop or mobile phones like iPhone), the user downloads and installs the program. The code is stored on their hard drive (yes, even your smartphone has a hard drive). With web applications, the code is not installed, it is simply run inside a web browser. When a user runs a web app on their smartphone, they are really running a web browser (the web browser is already installed on the phone) that interprets the web application's JavaScript code in order to do something meaningful. Figure 1-5 shows screenshots of a web app running inside a mobile browser and also a native app running on the mobile operating system. The full ramifications of this distinction are likely not very clear at this point. Never fear, clarity will come soon.

Figure 1-5 A web application running inside a mobile browser and a native app (the Calculator app) running on iOS. A web application can have the browser address bar hidden and home screen icon with the proper code added.

Now we're going to quit talking about desktop computers and their programs and focus on mobile application development. From now on, "native" will refer to either the programs written for the iOS or Android operating systems in their native languages. Unfortunately, learning both native programming and web programming is a bit too daunting for most people. Trying the "learn everything" method requires an extreme amount of studying and practice.

Picking either native or web programming is a much more tractable problem. We're going to explore the learning curve for these two approaches to help you decide which path is best for you.

Learning Native App Programming

As stated in the beginning of this chapter, native applications are programs that are written in the programming language specified by the maker of the smartphone. There are two major players, iPhone, and Android. IPhone programming uses the Swift language and Android uses the Kotlin language.

Unfortunately, learning the programming languages alone is not enough to build native apps, you also need to learn about the environment which executes the code you write (which in the case of native apps, the environment is the underlying operating system). The environment frameworks provide thousands of **functions** (a.k.a **methods**) you use to build your programs. Although knowing each and every method is not necessary, a healthy familiarity with many of them is required. This familiarity takes time to acquire.

You will also need knowledge of the "view" components provided by the operating system. If you look at an application window on a laptop or desktop, for example, there are three familiar buttons in one of the corners: close, minimize, expand. On Apple these are red, yellow and green buttons. The whole window (the way it looks and operates) and those buttons are part of the operating system. Similarly, iOS and Android have their own application windows and controls with which native applications can interact. Figure 1-6 shows some common user interface elements.

When we include the operating system methods and view components we get a more complete picture of the learning curve required for native programming. For iPhone programming, for example, the required topics include Swift, iOS, Cocoa Touch, and Xcode. Android programming requires a similar learning curve.

Figure 1-6 The environment frameworks provide the look and feel for some common components of applications like switches, sliders and tabs. These default styles can be overridden by code you write to make your app look anyway you desire. Because of the amount of graphic design and code required to make things look good in both web and native apps, many people utilize component libraries built by professionals.

The advantage of learning a native language is that all of the smartphone functionality is easily available to your code without any shims or outside libraries, and native apps have the best user experience design. This means they operate how app users expect them to operate, and that is no small advantage.

The biggest drawback of native programming is that after expending a large amount of effort to learn one path, your application will only be available for install on one manufacturer's device (either iPhones or Android phones, code for one will not run on the other). You might wonder if you can learn both, and the answer is yes, but it would be a very long road to take. Swift and Java are different languages, although they, like all programming languages, do share the basics of programming and object-oriented programming.

Only you can decide if the downside of only programming for one manufacturer outweighs the benefits of native programming. To help you decide, let's now look at the path to mobile development that uses web technologies.

Learning Web Programming

If native apps provide the best usability, why would anyone write a web program? The answer: web programs run anywhere, on any device with a web browser. Learning web programming is arguably easier than native development due to the environment provided by the web browser. So with relative ease you can learn how to write programs for anything, accessible from anywhere. Perfect, right? Not so fast.

Historically, for security reasons, applications running JavaScript in a web browser were not able to access the smartphone's camera, accelerometer, GPS, microphone, and other features. If JavaScript were able to access them, accidentally clicking a shady link in your smartphone could download spyware that could use your camera or microphone secretly! Obviously, this is a big concern and must be addressed (it is addressed by having the browser ask permission to access these features).

The second concern is usability. Web applications are designed with HTML and CSS. While CSS3 is a considerable improvement over it's predecessor, it still lacks some features graphic designers crave. Many believe that native applications "look and feel" better than web applications. This is partly due to native apps ability to access the slick graphic and user interface design provided by phone manufacturers, and partly due to better performance and lack of undesirable browser default behaviors.

These security and usability concerns mean that if a programmer wants to build an application that operates securely and looks good on the web and both major smartphones, he or she would have to learn three different programming languages: Swift for iOS, Kotlin for Android, and JavaScript for browsers! What a drag! Later we will see a solution to this problem.

Native and Web Programming Commonality

Now that we know the specific pros and cons of learning native versus web programming, let's talk about what they have in common. All three paths will require you to learn the following:

- Basics of programming (if/else statements, loops, etc.)
- Object oriented program design
- User experience design
- Serverside programming or serverless management
- Basics of computer networking

These are topics you can learn before deciding whether to be a native or web programmer. This is not to say that you must learn those topics before moving on—indeed, if you follow the path recommended in this book you will likely learn some of them as you learn JavaScript as opposed to reading separate, dedicated books to each of those topics. This book covers serverless management and computer networking to some extent.

To continue to topics beyond those listed above you must first decide whether you want to learn how to build a device-specific native application, or a web based application. The learning curve, the books you buy, and the websites you visit, and the languages you will learn will vary greatly based on the choice of path you take here. This book recommends learning web app development first, and then makes suggestions for further learning. This book does not intend to convince you of the merits of this path, but rather intends to educate you quickly, and as you work through this book you will gain the knowledge required to make the best choice for yourself.

Two Sides of App Programming

As illuminating as the previous discussion of the mobile app types was (or not!), there is more to most mobile apps (whether native or web) than the part you see on your phone.

Some applications, like a calculator app, are completely self-contained and do not require a server, unless you want to build a social calculator app to share your calculations with your friends! But many, if not most, applications written for mobile are social. They require accounts to login, and have features that allow the user to chat with other users, share photos and content or otherwise engage with other mobile phones. These applications, in addition to needing the **front-end** code that the user sees and interacts with, also require a serverside program, or **back-end**, which stores user login information, profile pictures, chats, and anything else necessary. When two users of your application want to chat, for example, the chats do not go directly from smartphone to smartphone. Instead, the application on Sally's smartphone uploads the message to a server. The server then notifies Tim's smartphone via a push notification or email. Tim then responds in the same manner. This process is shown in Figure 1-7.

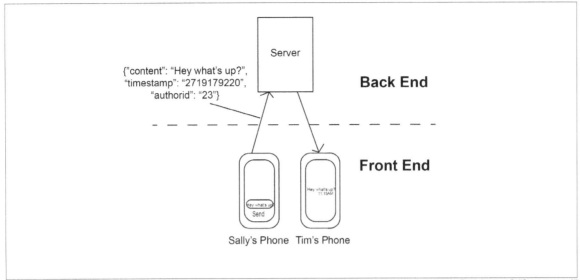

*Figure 1-7 How mobile apps send a message between two users, and the definition of "front-end" and "back-end" code. Files stored on the smartphone are called **local** files. Files on the server are called **remote** files.*

A Quick Note

Just to clear up possible confusion, one of the chief distinctions between native and progressive web applications outlined previously was the location of the application folder that holds the code files. It resides on the mobile device for native apps, or on a server for web apps. This may lead a newcomer to believe that servers are only required for hosting web apps, but although native apps are installed and stored on the smartphone's hard drive (not on a remote server like web apps) they still may *exchange data* with a server at some point, as shown in Figure 1-7. Native apps often have features (like social networks or multi-player games) that require a server. In the next chapter we will define "data" more exactly.

With this in mind, the question of whether or not your app needs a backend server should be clearer. This book will define exactly what a server is in Chapter 4, so don't worry if that concept is a little hazy at this point. If your application gets popular, a single backend server may not be enough: popular apps use server farms (a.k.a. data centers) containing hundreds of servers. Fortunately, services like the Google Cloud (https://cloud.google.com) allow you to rent servers so you do not have to buy hundreds of physical servers and put them in your basement. You turn on, log into, and program the cloud servers from your home computer or laptop terminal application. Cloud computing allows you to operate dozens or even hundreds of servers without ever touching them. Cloud computing is discussed in Chapters 4 and 5.

A Roadmap

If you are completely overwhelmed at this point, fear not! This chapter intended to throw a lot at you but don't worry if you didn't catch it all. We will go through each of the concepts in detail over the next several chapters. For right now, let's take a look at the big picture and see how all of these computer acronyms and terms relate in one big roadmap.

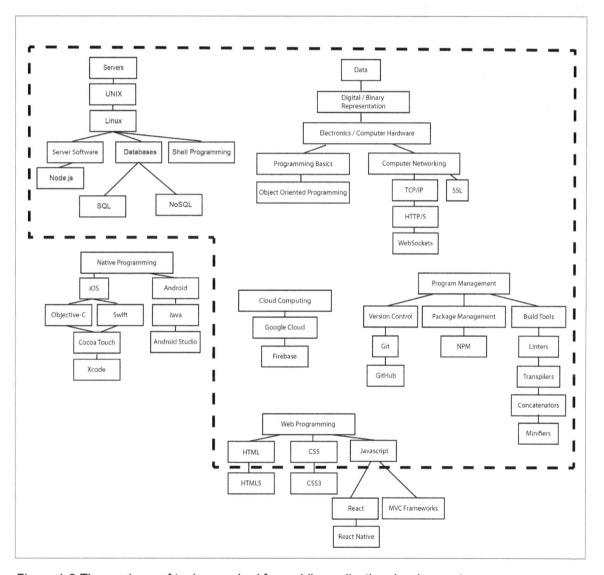

Figure 1-8 The roadmap of topics required for mobile application development.

What This Book Covers

Everything within the dashed lines in Figure 1-8 will be covered briefly in this book. As mentioned in the Preface, the purpose is to cover these topics (the background or prerequisite knowledge) as quickly as possible so that you can focus on learning to program mobile and web applications.

What You Need to Learn Elsewhere

Everything outside the dashed outline in Figure 1-8 are topics you will need to learn in depth on your own. Chapter 6 will recommend resources for each step of this path. The reasons for this path are explained later in the book, and it is completely an opinion. This book will serve as a useful prerequisite regardless of the path you take.

Review

In this chapter we learned that an application is a folder full of files, containing one special file that can be "run". In native programming, whether for desktop / laptop computers or smartphones, this file is called an executable or binary file. In the web programming world, this file is typically called index.html and it is interpreted by a web browser. In either case, the file links to the other files in the folder, which could be images, icons, configuration files and other files.

We learned that native applications are installed by copying this folder onto the user's smartphone hard drive. In contrast, we learned that web applications keep this folder on a server where it is publically accessible to any computer or smartphone connected to the Internet. We noted that both web and native applications often communicate with a server to store and update data.

We learned there is more to a mobile application than just the front end on the smartphone. Often, a server serves as an intermediary for data exchanged between users of an application. We learned how popular apps require many servers (that are often rented from a cloud computing company and accessed over the Internet).

Finally, we looked at a roadmap of nearly all application development topics and how they relate to one another. We illustrated what this book would cover, and what it would not cover.

In the next chapter we will learn more about data and the role programming languages play in marshaling it from place to place.

Chapter 2
What Does An App Have To Do?

In this chapter we will answer the question, "what does the code in an app have to do?" Now that we know an app is a folder of files, let's learn more about what the code in those files does. At first you may wonder how we can possibly answer such a general question, as apps have such different functionality. Surprisingly, despite the fact that apps like Instagram and Facebook and others do different things, the code underneath them shares a lot in common. We will define the commonality by doing the following things:

- Defining the concept of data
- Defining databases
- Viewing the world as digital data
- Looking at the two main types of code blocks
- Introducing the 3 languages of web programming
- Building a super simple web app to see the 3 languages in action

When we think about a photo sharing app for example, it may not be clear to a non-programmer what the application code has to do. In fact, learning what the app code has to do will first depend on learning what it *doesn't* have to do. In other words, we have to learn about what the environment provides. Remember from Chapter 1 that the environment differs slightly depending on whether we are programming a native or web app, but they both provide more or less the same functionality. We are going to learn both what our apps have to do, and what they don't, by looking at different types of data.

Data

The fundamental task mobile apps accomplish is shuttling data between smartphones and servers. But what is data? **Data** is a general term for any piece of information. Your name is data, as is your age, your email address, or your profile picture.

A **database** is simply an electronic storage of data. Databases are often designed in terms of tables, such as a table containing the information of the users of your app. It might look like the table in Figure 2-1.

User ID	Username	Email	Password	Blocked	Last Login
1	dude68	dude@trueanomaly.com	ksalk2984iusf	0	7284783739
2	jane273xl	jane@trueanomaly.com	lkaskf89s72k9c	0	7337478393
3	Kay282xkw	kay@trueanomaly.com	98asiofkccik	0	8363849944

Figure 2-1 A users table in a sample database.

A comment that you write on someone's social media post is also data. Along with the comment content, a database comments table should store the time it was posted and the user ID of the user who posted it. Database servers are simply computers connected to the Internet for the sole purpose of serving the data they store. By "serving" we mean responding to queries from devices. Crafting these **queries** is one of the main jobs of mobile app code (that's the code that you will write as a developer).

We mentioned previously that your profile picture is data. Actually, your profile picture is a piece of complex data, in that it is a file containing millions of pieces of data, each piece contains the color information of just one pixel on a screen.

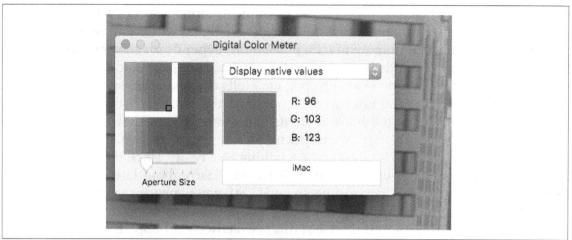

Figure 2-2 Pixel color values represented as three numbers, one for red, one for green, and one for blue.

Every picture is composed of pixels, each pixel is a combination of three colors: red, green, and blue. If we assign a number to represent the quantity of each color in each pixel of the photograph, we essentially get three two-dimensional matrices of numbers (one matrix for each color), that, when converted to binary, a computer can send to a monitor to convert into a visual image. The **RGB** values that form a single pixel are shown in Figure 2-1 from the Digital Color Meter tool available in the Applications->Utilities folder on Mac OS X.

Every number can be expressed in binary, which is a base 2 representation of numbers. Our common decimal system is base 10, meaning every 10 numbers bounces up to the next digit. When we convert all of these color value numbers to binary, package them together along with some metadata (like a file name, and size) we have created a basic image file. Common image file types are .jpg, .gif, .png, and others. These file types tell your computer how to unwrap and interpret the data. Although it is possible to put the binary data of an image in a database (as a **BLOB** datatype), it is more common to package it as a file and make it available for download from the server.

Let's take a moment to talk more about bits and binary data.

Bits and Programming

What is a bit? A **bit** is a voltage pulse on a wire that represents a "1" or a "0". The exact voltage can vary; some electronics use +5V to represent "1" and 0V for "0". You also see electronics books call "1", HIGH, or ON, and "0", "LOW", or "OFF", but they mean the same. When we combine bits together (for example, 10010111) we get a **byte**, or a digital word. Just like some words have multiple meanings, digital words can represent many different things, and like homonyms, their meaning depends on the context. Without context, digital information is just zeros and ones. Bytes are packaged into an envelope known as a file. The file type (e.g. .jpg, .png etc.) tells the operating system the context under which to interpret the information contained therein, much like the cover of a book notifies the reader of the book content. The example byte shown previously can represent the base 10 number 151, or a character on a keyboard, or a shade of Red, Green, or Blue for a single pixel on a monitor, or anything else really, since it is just a number. Figure 2-3 shows a snippet of HTML (which we will learn about later in this chapter) converted to binary digits. After reading about HTML you may want to refer back to this figure. It is a little odd to think of converting letters to numbers, such as converting a name into a **string** of zeros and ones, but this is exactly what happens when you type a key on a keyboard and see the letter displayed on your monitor.

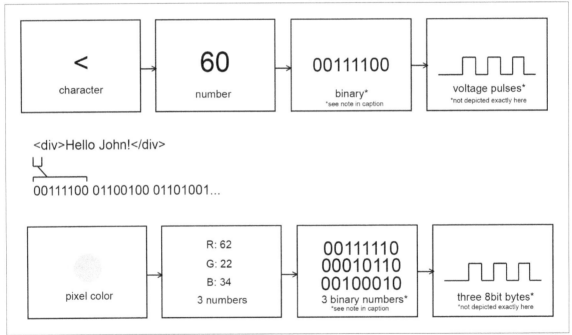

Figure 2-3 Bit equivalents of a section of HTML and a single pixel color value. The single "less than" character takes up one byte, or 8 bits. The RGB color value takes 3 bytes. *This is a simplified depiction of the process of converting a character to bits that are stored in memory on the computer hardware. For a more detailed and accurate description of how characters are encoded and stored in memory see a computer science textbook.

Every key on the keyboard, every letter or grammatical symbol we use to communicate can be converted to a binary number through character encodings. One common set you will use in the United States is called **UTF-8**.

When you finish your first programming book, you may be surprised at how few things computers can actually do. Computers can: do arithmetic, evaluate logical comparisons, and repeat any combination of the previous two tasks over and over. How can those three simple tasks combine to produce photo editing software, for example? The answer is, photo editing software depends on a lot of technology layers. A digital camera turns analog light into bits, then it packages those bits in a readable file. The operating system and hardware provide the link between the SD card or USB stick and a file that the software can read. Photo editing software can then manipulate the zeros and ones to produce cool filters and other effects, and then the new data is fed to a graphics card to turn into a displayable image on your monitor.

It takes a while to view the whole world as digital data, but as you can see, a lot of these conversions are done by hardware and software that your apps can depend on. And if it still seems overwhelming right now, don't worry, you won't be writing the next photo editing program just quite yet. This example is only provided to start your brain thinking in this way.

What an App Does and Doesn't Do

Fortunately, mobile app developers do not have to reinvent things. Our app code does not have to convert everything into zeros and ones. That conversion is done by lower level programming languages, and then by **assembly language**. Also, your app code does not have to deal with complex logic of converting analog waveforms from the microphone or camera into digital bits. As you might imagine, programming lower levels of the stack (or designing hardware) requires a much more detailed understanding of electronics, computers, and information theory. These lower layers combine to form the **environment** for the code for our app.

Our app can simply receive an image or audio file from those sources—the environment provides this bridge—then write code to manipulate it as desired. For programming nearly all mobile apps, it is sufficient to have a top level understanding of how computer code and data become bits on a wire rather than the ability to build circuits out of silicon that actually do that. App programmers do need to know Swift, Java, or JavaScript, which are higher level programming languages. So if lower level languages, the OS, and the web browser handle the difficult tasks, what does our code have to do?

Our programs will be event driven, which means our code will do a lot of nothing until a user clicks, swipes, or taps. These actions and others are called **events**. Then the code will respond appropriately to that event.

Our code will have three main tasks: marshaling data to and from the server, updating the view, and handling user events. One main task of our code will be data handling, this code is typically called the **CRUD** code (create, read, update, destroy). This corresponds directly to our users' actions. If they write a comment, our code will "create" it by storing it on the database server. Our code on other users' phones will "read" the comment from the database, and then display it. If the person who wrote the comment edits it, our code will "update" the server, and likewise, if the person deletes it, our code will "delete" it from the server. Figure 2-4 shows this process.

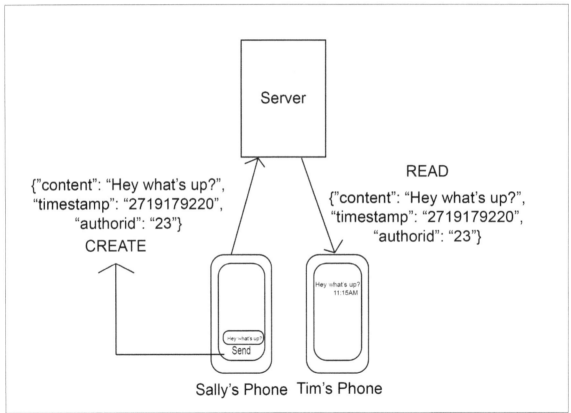

Figure 2-4 CRUD code in action. Pressing the "send" button on Sally's phone creates the record on the database server. Tim's phone reads the record from the database when Tim opens the app (possibly after receiving a push notification). The goofy format of the data with brackets and quotes is called JSON, we will learn more about it in later chapters.

Surprisingly, the majority of the code of the app will not be data handling, but will be handling user events, keeping track of state, and making sure the users do what we want them to do and nothing more. We discuss this next.

Dealing With Human Users

If we call data handling "CRUD", the code to deal with human users is "SLOG" (not an acronym or industry term, just a word that sounds equally as bad). This is the code that makes our app look good, makes it intuitive, and makes it unbreakable when faced with users who will inevitably use our app the wrong way (intentionally or mistakenly), and updates the state. CRUD does the action (uploads their profile pic) but SLOG code gives the user feedback (success or failure). CRUD applications would not be very friendly without SLOG. Unfortunately, SLOG takes up far more lines of code than CRUD ever will. Let's look at some examples of what SLOG code does.

First off, what do we mean by "tracking the state" of the app? Apps have many different states, and the state of the app will determine what the user sees. For example, nearly every app presents different features when a user is logged in. Or, if viewing a list of chats, when users click on a specific chat, that becomes the active chat, and naturally they would expect any messages they type in and send will go to the chat they have selected. Our app might have one component that reads the chats and another that posts the messages. Only by keeping track of the **state** can we make sure that all of our components are in sync. For example, it would be very frustrating if our chat app displayed messages from a chat with Susie, but when you type a new message in the input and press send it posted to a chat with George! Our chat app would get poor reviews for sure! Our app prevents this by keeping track of the "active chat", and all CRUD code in your components will reference it. In this case, the "active chat" is part of the state.

We wouldn't want to accidentally unfriend someone with a stray finger swipe right? Obviously, we should warn the user with a confirmation dialog if he or she is about to do something permanent like this. Dialogs, also called modal windows, are a common element of user interfaces. They are shown along with other common **user interface** (UI) components in Figure 2-5. Our SLOG code (the stuff we actually write) will handle the logic behind displaying, styling, and hiding UI elements, and our CRUD code will keep the server up to date on any changes that are made to the app state. Once the server is updated, our SLOG code may notify the user of success or failure (i.e. messages such as "chat message failed to post" or "you started following Yoshi").

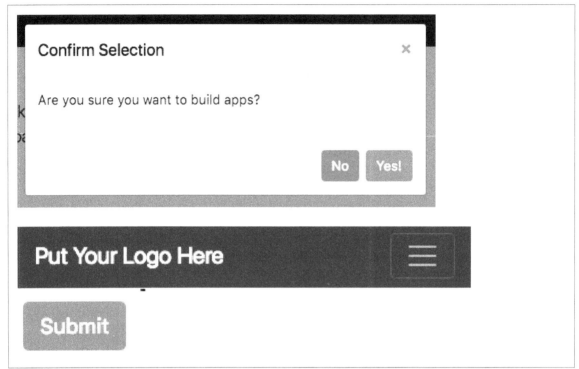

Figure 2-5 Modals, navbars, and buttons are all common UI elements.

The following is a typical workflow of the code we will actually write as a mobile developer. If we want to get the user to enter their first name, for example, we present them a text input to type into, and once they have done that, the SLOG code validates the user input, that is, it makes sure the data the user is supplying matches the data we expect. We don't want an email address entered as someone's first name. We listen for a click on the submit button, and when it happens, the CRUD code sends the data to the server, and when the server responds successfully, the SLOG code updates the state of app so that all components know where we stand, and the SLOG code presents some sort of dialog to tell the user if the upload was successful or if something went wrong.

We can never assume the user will know how to use our app, or that they won't try to deliberately break it. A voting app is a classic example. For web apps, the JavaScript code is visible and mutable, so the only way to ensure a user votes only once is with server side validation. We will talk more about this in Chapter 4.

SLOG code implements the User Experience (UX) design. UX designers attempt to answer questions such as the following:

- How will we cram so much information on such a small screen?
- How will the user interact with this?
- What hides the menu?
- What shows the menu?

We mentioned in the first chapter that one of the advantages of native code is that it makes UX design easier, as Apple and Google have built user friendly controls like buttons and toggles that you can use. Building good looking controls and interfaces in HTML and CSS can be tricky, especially if you are a solo programmer, since you get to be the programmer and the UX designer. Lucky you! Fortunately, we will see in Chapter 6 a way that web programmers can build apps that use native components.

Regardless of the type of mobile app you are building it will likely have CRUD and SLOG code. As we mentioned at the beginning of this chapter, apps that have very different end uses still share a lot of common code underneath. This is because the code the writes and receives data to and from the server (the CRUD) as well as a good portion of the user interface code (showing and hiding modal windows, menus, navigation bars and other SLOG) is all the same.

Building Blocks of Web Applications

In the preface it said that this book would present a biased path forward. Well the time has come for the bias. We will now overview HTML, CSS and JavaScript, which are the basis for web applications, and not native applications. Even if you think you may go the native programming route later on, I encourage you to read on, as the following chapters will provide good information that is general and brief enough to not waste your time. One of the great things about web programming is that you already have the tools to practice it. All you need is a plain text editor and a web browser. Both of these are installed on every operating system by default: on Windows, Notepad is the text editor and Internet Explorer is the default browser, on Mac OS X, TextEdit is the text editor and Safari the default browser. Unfortunately, depending on your setup, TextEdit may require some changes to the preferences to create what we are trying to create here, so before you start this, go ahead and download Sublime Text 3 (https://sublimetext.com). See Chapter 7 for more on this. The source code for these examples is available on this book's GitHub page, although I recommend typing them for practice (https://github.com/trueanomaly/selftaughtweb).

HTML / CSS

HTML is the Hypertext Markup Language. When reading "hypertext" just think: text sent over the Internet. A **markup language** is a language with tags that tell a computer what the content is. An example is below:

```
<p>This is a paragraph.</p>
```

The "p" in between "less than" and "greater than" symbols is called a **tag**. Tags tell the computer that what lies between, in this case 'p' means the content should be displayed as a paragraph. A markup language is computer readable, meaning that the computer can recognize the pattern of opening tag->content->closing tag and target that content, read it, change it, delete it, etc. If you wanted to change the color of the text in the second paragraph to red, you could tell a human, "turn the second paragraph text red." But a computer wouldn't know what to do, unless you marked up the content as shown below.

```
<p id="paragraph2">Hello world.</p>
```

Because the content is "marked up" the computer can **parse** it (read it) and find the paragraph with the ID **attribute** of "paragraph2" and change the color appropriately. Note that computers interpret things very strictly, and misplaced <, /, or ", can make the computer unable to understand the content.

CSS is a plain language that applies styles to the HTML. The HTML contains the <link> tag that tells the browser the file path to the CSS file that contains the styles.

Now let's try this. Create a new folder on your desktop and name it anything you want. Inside that folder, create two files, one named index.html and one named style.css. You create these files using a plain text editor. Check out Chapter 7, if you don't know what that is. Open your text editor, create a new file and copy in the code from Figure 2-6 into the index.html file and save it. Then open a new file again, copy in the code from Figure 2-7 and save it as style.css. Double click on the index.html file and it should open up in a web browser by default. If it doesn't, right click and tell it to open with your web browser.

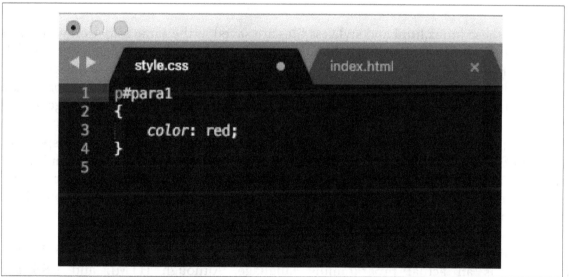

```
1   <!DOCTYPE html>
2   <html>
3   <head>
4   <link href="style.css" rel="stylesheet" />
5   </head>
6   <body>
7   <p id="para1">Paragraph 1.</p>
8   <p id="para2">Paragraph 2.</p>
9   </body>
10  </html>
```

Figure 2-6 Code for index.html. Ignore the DOCTYPE, head, body and html tags for now.

Figure 2-6 shows the markup typed into Sublime Text. Save the file as index.html.

```
1   p#para1
2   {
3       color: red;
4   }
5
```

Figure 2-7 Code for style.css. This code says, "find the paragraph with ID of 'para1' and color the text red."

Figure 2-7 shows the CSS typed into Sublime Text. Save the file as style.css.

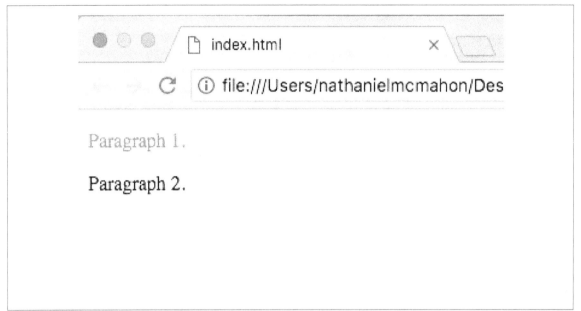

Figure 2-8 The result of opening index.html in a web browser. Clearly the paragraph 1 has the style applied to it.

As long as these index.html and style.css files are saved in the same folder on your hard drive, double clicking index.html should open a web browser and display the result shown in Figure 2-8. The web browser can read the <link> tag, find the style.css file on your hard drive, read the code in the file and apply the styles to the appropriate paragraph in the index.html file. Congratulations, you created your first web page!

CSS gets quite complex when trying to create layouts, especially layouts that respond to the size of the device. This type of CSS is called **responsive web design**, and it is a subject in and of itself. Don't worry if this example left you a bit lost. Entire books and courses are dedicated to the subject of HTML and CSS. Chapter 6 will show you where to find them.

The third component of web applications is JavaScript. Unlike HTML and CSS, JavaScript is an actual programming language. Although HTML and CSS are colloquially referred to as "code", JavaScript is the real "code" that powers the application. JavaScript, like all programming languages, can handle arithmetic, loops and basic logical statements that control the program flow. JavaScript can be included right inside the HTML file, but is most often contained in separate files and linked to the HTML much like we linked style.css to the our index.html file.

A Web App Example

To get our feet wet we will now create a web application that has two number inputs and a button that, when pressed, will multiply the two numbers together and display the result.

First we will create the **view**, which is programmer speak for the graphical part that the user can see. In web programming, the view is created with HTML and CSS. For this example we will create two inputs and a button, and a section to display the result. Open a new folder on your desktop and name it whatever. Then open a new file in your text editor and copy in the code from Figure 2-9. Save it as index2.html inside your new folder. Create a new file again and copy the code from Figure 2-10 and save it as app.js in the same folder.

```
index2.html                    ✕
1   <!DOCTYPE html>
2   <html>
3   <head>
4   </head>
5   <body>
6   <input id="numone" type="text" />
7   <input id="numtwo" type="text" />
8   <button id="multiply">Multiply Them</button>
9   <div>Result:</div>
10  <div id="result-target"></div>
11  <script src="app.js"></script>
12  </body>
13  </html>
```

Figure 2-9 Index2.html file for our first web application. Note that it links to our JavaScript file with a <script> tag.

```
app.js
app.js                    ×
1
2  document.getElementById("multiply").onclick = function() {
3      var one = document.getElementById("numone").value;
4      var two = document.getElementById("numtwo").value;
5      var result = one * two;
6      document.getElementById("result-target").innerHTML = result;
7  };
```

Figure 2-10 App.js file that powers our web application logic.

The HTML file is straightforward. The tags mean exactly what they say, two inputs and a button. Notice they have ID attributes so that we can identify them in our JavaScript code later on.

App.js contains the code that performs the multiplication. JavaScript can be embedded in an HTML file between <script></script> tags or can be in an external file and loaded in with the <script src="filename.js"></script>. We did the latter just to get comfortable with it.

```
index2.html                    ×
ⓘ file:///Users/nathanielmcmahon/Desktop/l

2                    4                Multiply Them
Result:
8
```

Figure 2-11 Our web app loaded into a web browser.

Now double click on index2.html file and it should open in your default web browser and look like Figure 2-11. There's our app! Type in a couple numbers and try it out! The numbers that you type in and the result of the multiplication are **models** in programming speak, and the code that multiplies them is called a **controller**. We will encounter these terms later on. If you have any trouble getting these examples to run, download the source code from the book website and compare it to yours. Also note quotation marks copied from a word processor are not the same as quotation marks typed into a plain text editor. Small differences like typos can cause your code to fail to run. In Chapter 7 we talk about how to access a JavaScript console that shows the error messages. Search "enabling developer tools" for more information.

You may wonder what causes our app to look the way it does even though we did not specify any CSS code for it. The styling of the app shown in Figure 2-11 is the result of the default styles applied by a web browser to the inputs, the button, and the text. We would only need to include CSS if we wanted to change these styles, such as making the button big and blue, for example.

So how do we share our web app? Right now our app is stored on our hard drive, but to make it available to anyone, anywhere, we could upload the contents of our web application folder to a web server. Then people could find it by typing in the IP address of the server into their web browser address bar.

Don't worry if the JavaScript code makes no sense right now. This example only intended to define all three of the components of a web application and show how they are linked in an HTML file.

You may be a bit disappointed that our first web app didn't really do anything. It certainly didn't have any CRUD code that communicated with a server and the SLOG code didn't do much to make it user friendly. Never fear, however. We need to walk before we can run.

Review

We defined data and databases. We learned that we live in an analog world that must be converted to digital for computers to understand. We also learned that every piece of data, whether the color of a pixel in an image, or a key on the keyboard, needs to be converted to a number to input it into a computer. We learned that the numbers chosen to represent data are not random, but instead follow the rules set forth by character encodings and the specifications of image file formats. Fortunately, we learned that cards, drivers, operating systems, and browsers handle much of this conversion, which leaves our mobile app code free to handle easier tasks. We learned about how the environment (the context in which our code is executed) determines what features are available to our app code. The environment varies depending on whether we are working on a native app or a web app, but the functionality provided is very similar, even if the code that implements it differs.

We learned that apps shuttle data to and from the server as the data changes. We learned that this type of code is called CRUD code. We learned that in order to make the CRUD more friendly to human users, we have to design user interfaces. That task falls on the UX designer, although in small or solo development teams, the programmer and UX designer could be the same person. We learned that programming the interface (handling user taps and swipes, and updating the app state accordingly) often forms the bulk of the code of a mobile app.

We then learned about the three fundamental web languages and their purposes. We learned how to make an HTML file, style it with a CSS file and then view it with a web browser. Then, we learned the basics of programming and a little about JavaScript specifically. Finally, we put HTML and JavaScript files together in a folder, linked them with an index.html file and effectively created our first web application.

Now we are going to peek into the technology stack. While we discussed how files of code and images are composed of digital bits that a computer can read, modify, transmit and receive, we did not discuss the particulars of the transmit and receive part. In the next chapter we will learn about the Internet and how it allows computers to pass data back and forth, which forms the basis of nearly all mobile applications.

Chapter 3
How Do Apps Communicate?

The Internet is a bunch of computers connected with wires (or wirelessly). These wires allow computers to send billions of tiny digital bits—which are nothing more than short voltage pulses—to each other. It is then the receiving computer's job to translate these zeros and ones into something humans can read. How computers do this effectively is analogous to how two humans would communicate over long distance. The same problems arise, with the same solutions, as we shall see shortly. The following computer networking concepts are relevant to both web and native apps that exchange data with a server.

Let's say you (a person) wanted to communicate with another person using only a wire, or, for the sake of this analogy, a rope. You could send pulses down the rope by raising and lowering your end of the rope rapidly. But pulses are not words, and the person on the other end of the rope would be clueless as to the content of your message, unless you two had previously agreed on some sort of code, say, one pulse means "yes" and two pulses mean "no". Through such an agreement you have effectively established the beginning of a simple **protocol**. A protocol is an agreement to do things in a certain way, every time.

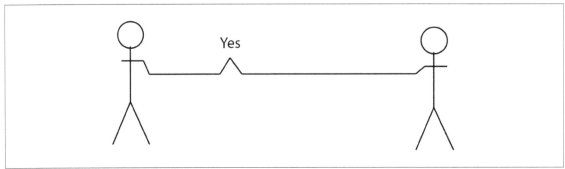

Figure 3-1 Communicating using pulses on a rope.

The problem with this protocol is obvious. Let's say you send one pulse to your friend. Your friend does not know if that single pulse is the whole message, or if she should wait for a second pulse. Perhaps you meant to say "no" with two pulses, but the instant after you sent the first pulse the smoke alarm sounded and you had to evacuate. Miles away your friend could not possibly know what happened, and now has no idea how to proceed. Did you say "yes", or are you in the middle of saying "no"? Clearly, our protocol is incomplete.

To improve our protocol, let's enclose the message in a three pulse envelope, as shown in Figure 3-2.

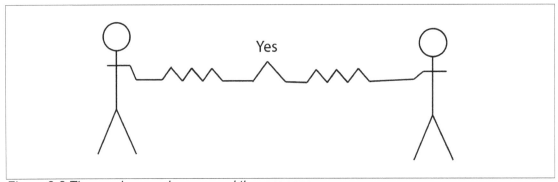

Figure 3-2 Three pulse envelope around the message.

Now if your friend receives three quick pulses, she knows to start listening until she receives three more quick pulses, otherwise the message is assumed to be incomplete. The three pulses must be distinguishable from the message pulses in duration or amplitude. This protocol is not perfect but it illustrates an important concept: the envelope. An envelope lets the receiving party know when the message is complete.

The Internet is built on a stack of protocols that ensure messages are sent and received properly. Due to the fractal-like complexity of computer networking, we will only cover the basics here. Each protocol encloses it's content in an envelope and takes care of one aspect of delivery. The stack layers are shown in Figure 3-3.

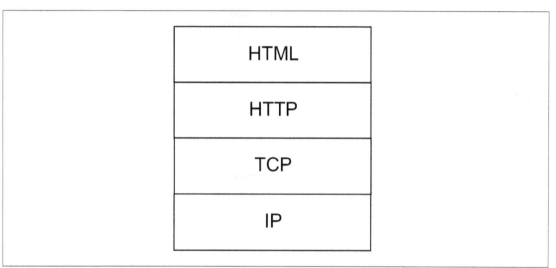

Figure 3-3 The protocol stack. In addition to HTML, other file formats sent on top of HTTP may include JSON or image files.

At the base, the **Internet Protocol** (IP) establishes addresses for computers (you may have heard of IP addresses). In fact, the colloquial phrase "connecting to the Internet" loosely means obtaining an IP address. It also handles packaging the data into packets. Above that the **Transmission Control Protocol (**TCP**)** acts as an envelope for the content to fix the same problem in the rope example previously mentioned. Above that, the **Hypertext Transfer Protocol** (HTTP) creates another envelope for the content that includes the response status and length, among other things. Finally, the HTML content acts as a final envelope for the actual content, using the structure <html><head></head><body></body></html> that we have already discussed in the previous chapter. It is common to use the metaphor comparing TCP/IP/HTTP/HTML to sending a letter in the mail. Figure 3-4 compares each of these protocol envelopes to the literal and figurative envelopes that enclose a business letter. The address on the envelope is the Internet Protocol. The envelope itself is the Transfer Control Protocol. The paper that the business letter is printed on is the Hypertext Transfer Protocol, and the format of the business letter is the HTML. Finally, we get to the content of the letter (the words of the message).

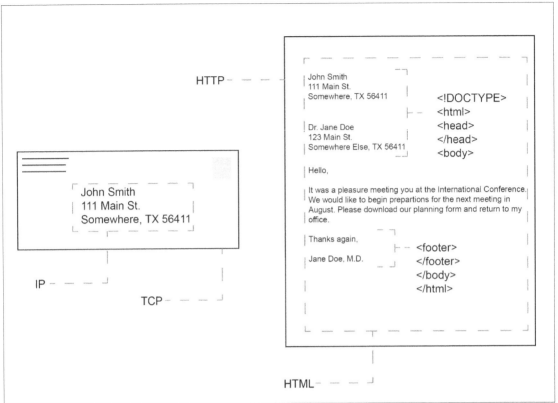

Figure 3-4 A business letter is enclosed by multiple "envelopes" that indicate the beginning and end of content.

This analogy is not only an extreme oversimplification, it isn't quite accurate: the Internet Protocol chops up the message into packets in a way that would be roughly analogous to putting the letter in the envelope, sealing it, using a paper cutter to cut it into chunks, resealing each individual chunk and writing the address on it and sending each one! The analogy definitely isn't perfect, but it's about as good an understanding as you need to have as a mobile developer, as every step just described will be handled by hardware and other code automatically and transparently to you.

It is not necessary for mobile developers to know every detail of the TCP/IP technology stack that forms the Internet (thank goodness!), as server and web browser software and networking cards do all of the wrapping and unwrapping. Nor is it necessary to know all of the academic abstractions of networking, from the various models of layers, and then the details of each layer, from the physical layer to the application layer. But, as always, the more you know the better, so search the web for details as desired. If you choose to learn more about any one part of it, your time would be best invested learning HTTP, and other parts of the **application layer**.

Internet Terminology

Although common usage interchanges the Internet and the web, the two are not synonymous. The Internet is about general computer networking (TCP/IP) and the web is about websites and web apps (HTTP, HTML).

Computers establish connections using **sockets**. Unfortunately, a true understanding of creating and binding sockets is a bit heavy, but can be pictured as a cable, or tunnel, connecting one port on each of the two computers, through which HTTP **requests** and **responses** can fly. A port is not a physical location on a computer but rather a concept created by the operating system that allows software programs to listen for messages coming in through the network card (whether Ethernet or Wi-Fi). Figure 3-5 shows this process.

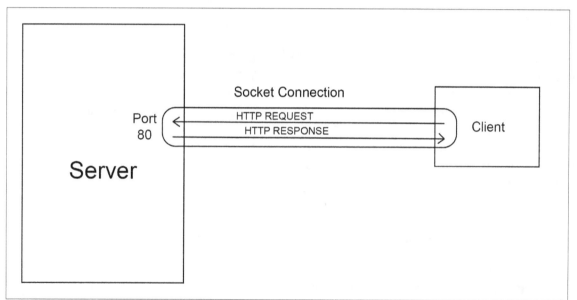

Figure 3-5 The creation of a socket connection between a web server and client. Not shown here is that native apps may open socket connections without HTTP, and WebSocket connections may remain open and skip exchanging additional HTTP headers for extra efficiency. A true discussion of TCP vs. HTML 5 WebSockets is beyond the scope of this book.

The Internet is composed of **servers** and **clients**. Clients send requests to servers, which issue responses. Clients can be mobile apps, web browsers, or command line utilities such as telnet, curl, or wget (more on command line utilities will come in Chapter 4). Web browsers are often called **user-agents**. For that term to make sense you can think of a web browser as your agent, making requests on your behalf. If you type in a website domain name into the address bar, your browser handles the complex details of making an HTTP request to the server much like human agents (real estate, talent, or travel) handle complex tasks for you.

Programs written for servers are often called serverside programs, and native or web apps are client side apps. It is possible, as you will learn later in this book, to write serverside functions in JavaScript using Node.js, but for now all we want is to understand the terms client, server, user-agent, request and response.

You may have noticed when you visit some sites your browser displays https:// in the address bar instead of http://. The extra "s" is for secure, and it means that the connection is using **transport layer security** to ensure that the data you are receiving is actually coming from the site you are on. This prevents **man-in-the-middle** attacks, and is especially important whenever you are sending or receiving sensitive information such as email addresses or passwords.

Domains

No doubt you have heard the term **domain** on television commercials for domain registrars and others. Domains are part of the **Domain Name System** (DNS). They are names that correspond with IP addresses. The database that stores the domains and their corresponding IP address is called a DNS server, and it functions like a phone book for computers. Why have a Domain Name System? Well, it wouldn't be very nice if you had to remember a number as the address for your local pizza shop. It is much easier to remember a name. Unfortunately, as mentioned earlier, computers like numbers, not names. The DNS functions as a bridge between human readable names and computer readable names. This concept should be familiar to you. Earlier, when introducing HTML, we talked about how markup languages make plain text content computer readable with the introduction of tags.

If your app idea is a mobile web and native app like Facebook, for example, then you will need a domain name for the web application. Even if you are only going to develop a native app, you may want a website to promote it, in which case you will need a domain for that. If you are building a native only app and don't need a promotional site, then all your app will need is a backend like Google Firebase, in which case the domain for your app will be provided to you when you create the project. We'll see more on that in Chapter 5.

Once you purchase a domain, you also have to ability to create any **subdomain** of it. For example, if you own trueanomaly.com, you can create go.trueanomaly.com. You can learn more about domain extensions, top level domains and DNS records with a web search, if desired.

Review Learning From Chapter 1

If some of the web versus native distinctions from Chapter 1 are still a bit hazy, we have enough information to clean them up now. When you open a web browser on your laptop, or mobile browser on your smartphone, and type in a domain, your browser will first contact a DNS server to find the IP address of that domain, then it will send an HTTP request to that IP address. The server will respond with the index file which will contain links to CSS and JavaScript code. Once your browser loads those links, you are now running the web app. From this point on, the web app will function nearly the same as a native app. The JavaScript code will listen for clicks and react to change the view (the HTML and CSS) accordingly. If you type in a status update and press send, JavaScript will grab the content of the update and shoot it off to the database for storage. Your browser will handle all of the nitty gritty details of packaging the update in IP/TCP and HTTP envelopes. The JavaScript code will simply listen for a response. If the browser notifies the JavaScript that the response was **HTTP 200 OK**, then the status update posted successfully, and JavaScript can now update the view (show it on your news feed). The first part of this process is shown in Figure 3-6.

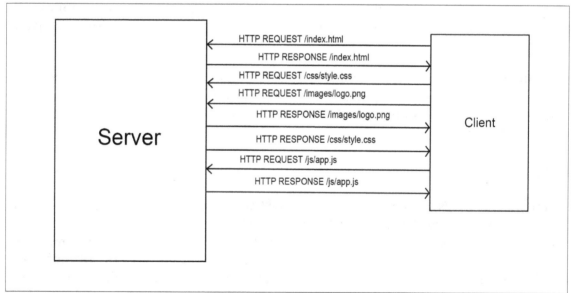

Figure 3-6 The process completed by a web browser requesting and receiving the content and code of a web application from a server. These individual requests/responses travel through one or more socket connections established by the web browser. The first request is for the .html file. Once received, the browser parses it and determines what images, JavaScript code, and stylesheets to request.

Web applications function within a browser (on a desktop or mobile phone). They have many of the same features as native apps (they can upload status updates, photos, etc.), however, there still differ from native apps in some key ways. Web applications are not installed, they reside on a server, from which the code is downloaded. They can be stored (cached) on the phone, you can even create a home screen icon for them, but this icon functions more like a browser bookmark than a native app icon. The code that runs the app is interpreted by a browser, it is not compiled and stored on your smartphone hard drive. Features like push notifications do not function the same as native app push notifications and other features linking to smartphone functionality work only with some browsers.

Because large companies put considerable value on a homogenous user experience (regardless of which smartphone or browser the users prefers) many choose to create native applications. Later we will talk about a solution called React Native that allows a programmer to use JavaScript to create a native app. This means that the application code is still JavaScript, and much of it works exactly the same as the JavaScript code that runs the web app, but the app has been packaged with some native code (that's the React Native part) that acts as a bridge between the smartphone and your code. One difference, however, is that the mobile app code doesn't request HTML/CSS from the servers. Instead, JavaScript code in the app requests data only, in JSON format, and then it populates the native views on the phone. Mobile apps (both native and web) use the same TCP/IP connections to servers. We will talk more about React and React Native in Chapter 6.

Hopefully this discussion along with the additional knowledge gained in the past two chapters has not confused you to the point of exhaustion. Realize that you may not fully understand these distinctions until you have built some apps using JavaScript yourself, so don't fret.

JSON

We mentioned JSON, now let's define it. **JSON** stands for JavaScript Object Notation, and it is a computer readable format for data, much like HTML, but unlike HTML, it is just data (no headers, paragraphs, divisions, etc.) It works as a **key value** system, which is a common programming construct found in **associative arrays**, **objects** and **NoSQL** databases. Don't worry if you don't know those terms, just realize that you will encounter key value concept a lot in your programming study. How it works is simple: if you provide a key, you get the value associated with that key. This is illustrated in Figure 3-7.

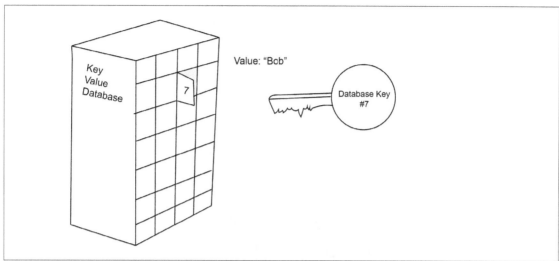

Figure 3-7 Key value system.

An example of JSON is shown in Figure 3-8. In the JSON shown in the figure, if you named the JSON string "data" you could get the user's name by calling data.username. Of course, that probably doesn't make a lot of sense to you right now, as we have not covered how to write code to get JSON data from a server or serverless backend. So don't worry, this is just to prepare for that discussion later on.

JSON Format:
{ "key" : "value" }

Example:
{
    "username" : "Bob64" ,
        "content" : "Hey there!" ,
    "timestamp" : "18181771891"
}

Figure 3-8 JavaScript Object Notation, a standard way to format data for transmission between servers and clients, even if you aren't using JavaScript. The JSON shown could represent a comment made by Bob64 being sent to a server for storage. JSON objects can have multiple keys and values. The keys here are username, content and timestamp, and their corresponding values are Bob64, Hey there!, and 18181771891.

Despite it's name, JSON makes no assumptions that your app is using web technology, and it can be used by code in native programming languages. Because JSON is an easy and unbiased way to exchange data with servers, it has become a de facto standard.

Review

This chapter did not intend to make you an Internet expert, but rather give you some insight into the absolutely massive technology stack that makes mobile development possible. This chapter summarized a huge amount of information very succinctly, perhaps too succinctly for those who like the full picture.

Both web and native apps communicate with servers to store data and do other tasks such as send emails and push notifications. Native apps are stored on the smartphone hard drive, so the only thing they send and receive is data such as picture files, comments, number of likes, etc. The textual data like comments and number of likes will likely be in JSON format, which is translated by the environment to a string of bits, packaged into each layer of the protocol stack, and sent through a socket connection.

Web applications exchange data with servers just like native apps, but before that happens the app code itself has to be sent to the browser. Each of the characters in the code files will be translated into bits, those bits will be sent along a wire to the user where the web browser will interpret them as computer code. That computer code will instruct the browser when, where and how to respond to any actions that the user takes (such as clicking the submit button on a comment field).

It will take some time for you to be able to visualize this, don't worry if it's tough right now. Fortunately, it is only required that an app programmer be aware that this is happening, it is not important to know the intimate details of each logical step, as these details are hidden away in the code of web browsers, server programs, networking cards, and the chips on the motherboards of both the server and the client! Your mobile app is simply the very top of the stack!

Chapters 1-3 Review

In the first chapter we learned that apps are folders of files that contain code that runs on computers, and that smartphones are mini computers with their own operating systems. The specific programming language used to write the code in the files depends on the operating system, and the operating system depends on the manufacturer of the smartphone.

We learned that two main types of apps exist, native and web. Native apps are installed on the smartphone whereas web apps run inside a mobile web browser. The code files for native apps are stored on the smartphone hard drive, and for web apps the code files are stored on a remote server where they can be downloaded by a mobile web browser. The chief advantage of native apps is their inherent access to the smartphone features and their familiarity to most users. Web apps, on the other hand, are platform agnostic; they run on desktops and smartphones of any brand without the developer needing to learn additional languages.

Chapter 1 provided a roadmap of the world of web and mobile development. Web and mobile developers need only know detailed information about a very small subset of this roadmap. Web and mobile app development only require a rudimentary understanding of the other topics, and those are the topics covered in this book.

In Chapter 2 we started to wrap our heads around the abstract concept that everything we perceive with our five senses is in fact analog data that can be converted into digital data. Digital data is composed of bits, which are short voltage pulses representing zeros and ones, which—when strung together—form digital words, or bytes. These bytes are used to represent everything from pixel color values (that can form an image on a monitor) to characters (letters and grammar symbols) that can be read. These bits can be stored in computer memory or transmitted to other computers on wires or wirelessly. We learned that apps sit on top of a technology stack that provides an environment that makes writing app code easier.

In Chapter 3 we learned the very basics of computer networking, which is how apps communicate with servers. We learned that a massive protocol stack makes the Internet work, but thanks to lower level software, networking hardware, and the operating system, our apps will rarely if ever have to touch more than the top of this stack.

We did not cover wireless networks (either Wi-Fi or Cellular 4G networks) but these are simply more protocols stacked on top of the TCP/IP stack, and they function transparently to the app developer. In other words, your app need not distinguish data coming in on Wi-Fi from data coming in on the cellular network (although smartphones do allow your app to be notified when the network connection type changes).

Protocols act as envelopes that ensure complete delivery of data in the right order. Once the data arrives, standard character encodings and file types (defined by specifications that everyone agrees on) ensure the client can understand the content. Picture a book put into an envelope and mailed. The protocol is the envelope that gets the book to the proper place, the file formats and data specifications (the book cover) let the receiver understand what he or she received.

Chapter 4
What Are Servers?

In this day and age we have all heard the term server, but what is a server? A server is a computer, much like your home computer, but unlike your home computer it is always powered on and connected to the Internet. Most home computers get whatever IP address their **Internet Service Provider** (ISP) allocates, and this changes whenever they connect. A server, however, has a fixed IP address and is thus locatable at that address anytime, from anywhere.

To review, the only substantial differences (besides size and computing power) between a home PC and a server are as follows, a server:

- Is always powered on and wired to the Internet
- Has a **fixed IP address**
- Runs web server software such as **Node.js**

Can you turn your home PC into a server? Yes, with web server software you can, but it may take a bit of extra money to your ISP for a fixed IP address if you desire one.

Types of Servers

As mentioned in Chapter 1, most mobile apps use a server as a third party intermediary to store data uploaded by the app users, whether that data is comments, chat messages, photos, or whatever else. In the not too distant past this seemingly simple operation was a whole lot harder, as we will see in this chapter.

There are three main types of servers your mobile app can use: database servers, static / storage servers, and application servers. It is also quite common to create servers dedicated to specific, intensive tasks such as email, image processing, notifications, and

DNS, but we're going to focus now on the big three aforementioned types. Even though we will learn to prefer serverless backends to cloud servers in the next chapter, the information in this chapter is nonetheless relevant, as our app will not really distinguish between exchanging data with a server or serverless backend.

The Cloud vs. Physical Servers

You've probably heard of the cloud. The cloud is a bunch a servers working together to provide a continuous service. From the perspective of a developer, the cloud provides a way to create an array of backend servers that provide nearly flawless storage and hosting of your app data regardless of the amount of data or traffic. The cloud is built on the concept of **virtualization**, which is multiple computers using only partial resources to simulate one computer. This simulated computer is called a server **instance**. From the perspective of the developer (and our app users), the server instance is indistinguishable from a physical server, you still log into it, program it, backup it's data, etc. It still works just like a physical server, your app will exchange data with it the same way, and your app's users will have absolutely no idea what is going on behind the curtain. The principle advantage of cloud servers is that they can be turned on or off on demand, especially as demand changes, and there is no need to purchase expensive equipment, storage space, or wire things together. The cloud sure beats putting servers in your basement. This is shown in Figure 4-1.

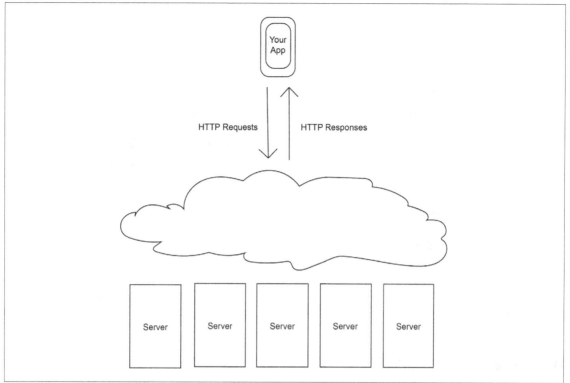

Figure 4-1 Server virtualization in the cloud can be visualized as a cloud floating above a bunch of servers. To the app above the cloud, it just appears like a single server. Whichever server handles the request becomes irrelevant.

Uniform Resource Locators (URLs)

Before we continue talking about servers, let's briefly define **URL**. You have probably heard the term URL. URLs are an address that allows a client to upload or download something (a resource) to or from a remote server. The resource could be an HTML web page, an image file, a document, a code file, or something else. The structure of a URL is shown in Figure 4-2.

Figure 4-2 A URL format; in parenthesis are some terms loosely equivalent to help you keep track of all this new terminology. There is more that can be included in a URL, such as username, password, and port numbers.

You can see that after specifying the protocol to be used, a URL starts with a domain name. The domain name is translated into an IP address as mentioned earlier so that example.com becomes a series of numbers separated by periods (e.g. 192.168.1.1). If you happen to know the IP address of a server you can type in that number instead of the domain name. Everything after the first forward slash after com is a **relative URL**, as it is relative to that domain. As we will see shortly, API endpoints are defined by their relative URLs.

Database Servers

We learned the definition of a database in Chapter 2. So what is a database server? No surprises here: a database server is just a database that is connected to the Internet and listening for connections. When a connection is made, the database waits for a query, and then returns the result of the query (which is the data requested).

SQL vs. NoSQL

There are two main types of databases, SQL and NoSQL. The former uses the Structured Query Language and the latter does not. SQL databases are structured in tables like we mentioned in Chapter 2. Each table has a particular content, like the users or comments table, and contains columns relevant to that content. Queries in SQL are written in plain English, but reading them out loud sounds a bit robotic. A typical SQL query looks like "SELECT * FROM users WHERE joined > 17162827292", and reads like "Select all the rows from the users table where the value of the column named joined is greater than May 31, 2017." In this case, the joined column contains a **UNIX Timestamp** for the date and time a user joined. UNIX Timestamps are the number of milliseconds since 1970, and are the common computer way of expressing dates.

In contrast to SQL databases, NoSQL databases do not have tables, rather, each piece of data in the database has a unique key, and upon providing the key, you get the value. See

Figure 3-7 in the last chapter as a refresher of this concept. NoSQL databases tend to be super fast and many are "evented", meaning they can take action when a particular piece of data changes. We will see later in this chapter and the next how this functionality (along with Firebases rules syntax) eliminates the need for a server side application to translate the data for our app.

```
/comments/8723138748792/  =>   {"content": "Hey there!", "timestamp":"1923488", "authorname":"Nate"}


/comments
    /8723138748792
        /content : "Hey there!"
        /timestamp: "1923488"
        /authorname: "Nate"
```

Figure 4-3 A NoSQL database is structured like a filesystem where each database entry has a unique URL. Accessing the relative URL /comments/8723138748792 causes the server to respond with the JSON on the right. The bottom of the figure shows the directory-like structure of the NoSQL database.

One drawback of NoSQL databases is that they are not **relational**, so they can't show the relationships between data. In the SQL query example earlier, we wanted to get a list of all the users who joined after a certain date. To do this, we crafted a query containing a WHERE clause. In a NoSQL database, there is no way to do this. We had better hope that we planned for the need for that data ahead of time! This is because the only way to get such data quickly or easily would be to create a separate piece of data that tracks it. If we hadn't been adding to a separate list everytime a user joined from May 31, 2017 onward, the only thing we could do to get this list is write a program to loop through every single user and look at the date they joined. If our database were large, this could be a very slow operation.

With an SQL database, this type of query is easy. In fact, we could query the data for any date, or query based on any other column, at any time. When using NoSQL it is imperative that you know before building your app what lists of data your app will need so that your code can write to those lists everytime it adds data.

Static / Storage Servers

Static, or storage servers provide a convenient way to store data of any type. They work similar to NoSQL servers in that a unique URL defines a unique piece of data. Most of the time, app programmers use these servers to put code files—whether HTML, CSS, or

JavaScript—as well as user uploads such as profile pictures or other files your app's users upload.

Although these static storage servers are indeed servers, cloud providers typically put a wrapper of code around them so you can easily upload and dump data in or out without worrying about a filesystem. The providers call these servers **buckets**, and typically you can view data, upload data, change data access rules, or dump data, through some sort of web interface, as well as programmatically through your app of course. When you upload data, the provider code returns the unique URL for the data. Any computer anywhere can then access it, according to the access rules you specify.

Application Servers

Application servers contain code scripts just like our web or native applications. The purposes of these scripts are the following:

- Authentication
- Authorization
- Validation
- Sanitization
- Secure Operations
- Hosting the App (for web apps only)

How can it possibly be so complicated, when all we want is a server to store our user chats in a database? Fortunately, in the next chapter we will see that these days it is nearly simple, but for now, let's talk about why it used to be complicated.

Let's say we want a database to store user chats. We'll put up a database server, give our app a username and password with privileges to do whatever in the database. Now our users can send messages to each other through the database. It all works beautifully until a malicious user deletes our database! By providing unlimited access credentials to any user of our app, we have created a massive security hole similar to a bank providing every account holder a key to the vault.

Simply storing data on a database server is not enough. In order for our app to function and stay secure, we need to know who is posting data (**authentication**), and whether or not they have permission to do so (**authorization**). In the past, the only way to do this was to put an application server in front of the database server and use it as a secure gateway. The application server ran scripts—short pieces of code written in a server language like PHP, and more recently Node.js—that determined who the user was (through **cookies**) and if they had permission to modify (create, read, update, or destroy) the content. Remember CRUD code from Chapter 2? Yep, CRUD code used to run on the application server too. If the user were valid and had proper permission, the application server would use the database credentials (which were stored on the server and not accessible to the app user) to connect to the database (through TCP/IP) and perform the query on behalf of the user. Then the application server would return the result to the user. This is shown in Figure 4-4.

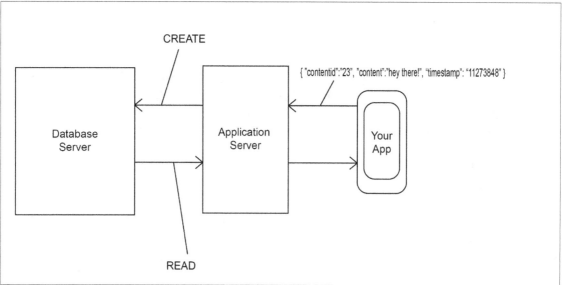

*Figure 4-4 An application server used for CRUD operations. For small apps the application and database server were often the same server. The application server simply connected to itself (an address called **localhost**).*

But authentication and authorization are not enough. We also want to make sure the data users are putting in our database is valid. We don't want birthdates in the username column, for example. This requires data **validation**, which is code to make sure that the data fits the format we are expecting for the database column it is destined for.

Next we must **sanitize** the data. Back before NoSQL, every database was SQL, and SQL has a major vulnerability known as an SQL injection. This happens when a bad guy puts SQL code in as their username, for example, and then our application server drops it into the query, not knowing that when the database server gets it, it will execute an entirely different query than the one we are expecting! This technique could be used to steal email addresses or any other data stored in the database. Sanitization is a process of using code on our application server to destroy any attempts to inject a query into the data. Fortunately, NoSQL databases do not have this vulnerability. However, even NoSQL databases can present a different security problem known as XSS, if their output is not filtered before being displayed in a different environment. We will mention XSS again later on.

The final task application servers perform is secure operations. These are operations that require credentials that we do not want publically available in our JavaScript code. Some examples include the following:

- Accessing a database on a remote server
- Charging a credit card
- Sending email
- Sending push notifications

All of these operations require interaction with a separate server, and those interactions will require credentials. If we stored the credentials for our credit card payment gateway in our JavaScript app, for example, then anyone could issue or reverse charges that appear to come from our app!

As an aside, remember in Chapter 2 in our first web app we linked the JavaScript code with a <script> tag in the index.html file? Well the code is visible to anyone and there is no way to hide it. Any passwords or other credentials put in JavaScript are visible in the clear to all users of our app! That is why some operations cannot be securely performed by JavaScript apps. In those cases, we need an application server, or, as we will learn in the next chapter, serverless functions.

Application Programming Interface

An application programming interface (API) is a way for computer programs to interact with each other. APIs are what allow code to interact with something programmatically, that is, without human intervention. For example, when you want directions, you might type an address into the Google Maps app. That works great, but what if you want your app to get directions? Your app doesn't have it's own iPhone and a set of fingers. Instead, your app will use code that you write to formulate a request in a very specific format (specified by the Google Maps API documentation) that can be parsed by Google Maps servers. Your app will then get a response in a very specific format that you can use in your code. APIs are some of the most useful things we can learn as a programmers because they give our apps the power to leverage all sorts of functionality that we couldn't write ourselves.

Terminology Overload

At this point you may feel overwhelmed with the terminology. Fear not! Much of it is simply duplicated terms. The only things being sent over the Internet are the same IP/TCP/HTTP requests and responses mentioned in Chapter 3, but since these requests are often made to a serverside program that is hosting an API, they are often called API requests. API requests are normal HTTP requests, but have their content (a.k.a. data payload) written in a very specific format that the serverside program will expect, parse, understand and respond to appropriately. All HTTP requests are made to a URL, but if the URL is one that accepts or returns data from an API, it is called an API **endpoint**. Unlike the URL shown in Figure 4-2, API URLs do not end in a filename, they simply trigger code on the server to run. If these API requests are made from code written in JavaScript, they are often called **AJAX requests**. Almost inevitably, loose terminology leads to some people calling API endpoints "AJAX endpoints", but they are not different. API endpoints can be "consumed" by a client app written in many languages, not just JavaScript. These endpoints each have a particular URL scheme that indicates what data you are looking for. For example, if you request a specific comment associated with a piece of content, you might send a request to trueanomaly.com/posts/243/comments/12398282, where 243 is the ID of the post and 12398282 is the ID of the comment. Let's take a look at all of this together.

Old Architecture Example

An example of the architecture of a web / native app using a cloud server instance is shown in Figure 4-5. As shown in the figure, the application server acts as an intermediary between the database and the mobile or web application. The server here hosts a single API endpoint for posting and reading comments. The server differentiates between these two requests by parsing the request body. The figure shows just one sample endpoint but in a larger app there would be endpoints for each list of data the app would request. Requests are sent from the client side code on the app to the application server endpoints. Upon receiving a request at a particular endpoint, the application server would parse it to figure out what information was being requested, then it would craft a query the database server. Using the stored secure credentials (username and password) for the database, the application server would query it, then, upon receiving the results, would format the results into JSON and send them back to the client side app.

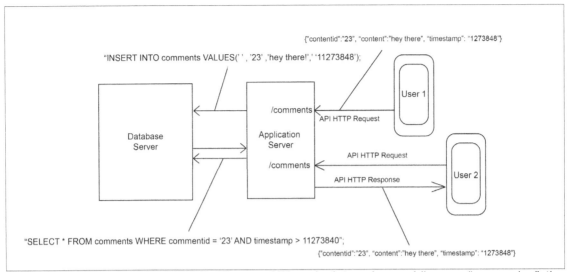

*Figure 4-5 Application backend hosting an API endpoint and a mobile app "consuming" those endpoints. The endpoint /comments is a relative URL that refers to **https://trueanomaly.com/comments** with the domain name omitted for clarity. The figure shows two separate requests: the top request posts a comment, the bottom request reads all the comments, in this case there is only one.*

This diagram shows that in the recent past, building a mobile app required programming not only the client app (in Swift, Java or JavaScript), but also the application server. The serverside program that parsed the request, crafted a query, and formatted the results as JSON was not automatic! Those programs were written in PHP or another serverside language. In this architecture, the application server often fulfilled multiple roles, in addition to hosting the data endpoints, like handling file uploads, images and profile pictures. The application server code could move these files to other servers for processing, compression and storage elsewhere.

Serverless backends, which are the subject of the next chapter, make a whole bunch of this programming as simple as clicking through a **Graphical User Interface** (GUI).

UNIX / Linux

Although servers can have any operating system (including Microsoft Windows or Mac OS X), UNIX and Linux servers dominate the Internet. We are only going to discuss Linux, as for our purposes, UNIX and Linux are the same thing, but don't say that to computer scientists! There are many different types of Linux; everyone has a favorite.

Linux is an operating system that can have a graphical user interface like Mac OS X or Windows, but is commonly used from the command line, and often remotely using a program called **SSH**. Linux is a lot of things to a lot of people, but it's easiest to think of it as three things:

- A filesystem
- A bunch of utility programs for programmers
- A server

Technically, if you're using a serverless backend, you won't need to learn much about Linux. However, there are some basic programming concepts that are best learned in a Linux environment. I would encourage you to learn as much about Linux as you can, as it will help solidify some of the hazy concepts from previous chapters, particularly about programming and networking. Nothing will get you more comfortable with files, executables, ports, domains, emails, package managers and many other tools than busting out a Linux textbook and hitting the command line! In addition, many source code bundles that you will utilize (such as Node.js or React) will use a package manager for installation. This package manager will run on the command line, so learning some basic commands will be helpful down the road.

Let's talk about the first aspect of Linux, the filesystem. If you have ever used a computer you have already interacted with a filesystem whether you knew it or not. A filesystem is just a hierarchy of folders (a.k.a. directories). All Linux variants have a slightly different directory structure, but roughly follow the same format. The forward slash (/) represents the bottom of the filesystem, known as the root directory.

```
Last login: Thu Feb 15 10:50:14 on console
You have mail.
Nathaniels-iMac:~ nate$ cd desktop
Nathaniels-iMac:desktop nate$ cd programming_book
Nathaniels-iMac:programming_book nate$ ls -a
.                    .DS_Store           chapter1            chapter3
..                   Back Cover.docx     chapter2            chapter4
Nathaniels-iMac:programming_book nate$
```

Figure 4-6 Moving around the filesystem in the Terminal app. Here we changed directories and listed the files within a directory.

Some of the folders hold programs that make up the operating system, others are for user installed programs. "Bin" is a common folder name, and it is short for binaries, which, as we mentioned in Chapter 1, is another name for executable files. Linux command line commands can be combined into **shell scripts**, which are programs that do a series of command line tasks automatically. Shell scripts can be triggered to run periodically by adding them to the **crontab**, which is a list of periodic tasks.

I believe poking around on the Linux command line gives the programmer a more tangible experience of programming, and a better feel for how computers really run. It may seem odd at first to think of everything on the computer as a file, but it's true, and unless you're a computer engineer, you won't have to worry about anything deeper than that.

In addition to a filesystem, Linux also contains a number of command line tools. Linux was developed with a toolbox for programmers. Linux has programs for searching for files, searching the contents of files for patterns, moving, copying, and deleting files, packaging files together as programs, installing packages of files, connecting to remote servers, and many other things.

Lastly, a computer running Linux can easily become a web server, an email server, an FTP server, a DNS server, or any other type of server you could need. It is built as a multi-user platform that contains a solid **file permission system**. Permissions are numbers or letters that indicate who can access, execute and modify files, and view, change and pass through directories.

All you need to turn a Linux box into a server is server software. Server software typically starts automatically when you boot up and binds itself to a port. You may remember ports from Chapter 3. It can be confusing when reading programming books—sometimes they use the term server to refer to the Linux box itself, other times to refer the software on the box that functions as a server (like Node.js).

If you use Mac OS X, you have been using an OS very similar to UNIX. Mac OS X is a pretty face (GUI and other changes) on top of a variant of UNIX. To get to the command line, open up the Terminal app in the Utilities folder. From there you can move around the filesystem, create and open files and even use SSH to connect to cloud servers. In that case your Terminal command line becomes the command line of the cloud server and you can execute commands as if you were plugged into it!

Even if you will never manage a server of your own, most real world apps require the installation of open source code, and this process will involve some basic Linux command line knowledge, including the shell, directories, file creation and deletion, and permissions.

A summary of this knowledge is listed below:

- Local versus global installation, PATH variable
- Navigating the filesystem (cd, mv, cp, rm)
- Creating and running simple shell scripts
- Basic utility programs (nano, cat, gzip)
- Installing code with npm or yarn
- Set file and directory permissions
- Understand processes and owners

Linux professionals are often called system administrators. They know how to add and remove users, install new software, secure servers with firewalls, and other things. Client side programmers do not need this knowledge, although it can be helpful.

Review

In this chapter we defined servers. We learned that they are just powerful versions of home computers that are accessible anytime at a known IP address. We learned the purpose of servers and the role they play in hosting and storing data for native and web apps. We learned that servers are often dedicated to specific roles and the cloud makes it somewhat easy to setup multiple servers dedicated to these roles. We learned the difference between SQL and NoSQL databases.

We then learned that application servers perform the following functions:

- Authentication
- Authorization
- Validation
- Sanitization
- Secure Operations
- Hosting the App (for web apps only)

Fortunately, web and native app programmers no longer need to accomplish the complex task of programming and administering servers, thanks to serverless backends. We learn about how they replace the need for physical or manually managed cloud server instances in the next chapter.

Chapter 5
What Is A Serverless Backend?

Serverless backends provide the same functionality as cloud or physical servers, just without the hassle. Just as cloud server instances were a vast improvement over having to own dozens or hundreds of physical servers, serverless solutions eliminate even more of the heartache, by removing the need to manage all those cloud servers. The term serverless is a bit misleading, as there are definitely servers back there, but you will have no responsibility for them, your code will simply interact with them.

Managing multiple servers is a serious chore. If your app grew to the point of having tens of thousands of users you would need a whole bunch of application and database servers to handle the traffic. Even though you wouldn't have to physically touch the cloud servers, you would still have to launch them, install and configure software on them, update the software, and program the servers to handle the data your app users upload. If one server went down you wouldn't want to lose any data, so another server would boot up to replace it, provision itself with your app code, and so on and so forth. This would require a large knowledge of server administration including writing separate server management programs (Perl, Python or shell scripts) to keep the servers up-to-date, in-sync, scaling, and backed up. Note that these are separate from the serverside scripts we talked about in previous chapters; these scripts are not for data handling, they simply administer the servers themselves. Whew! Figure 5-1 shows an example of this complexity.

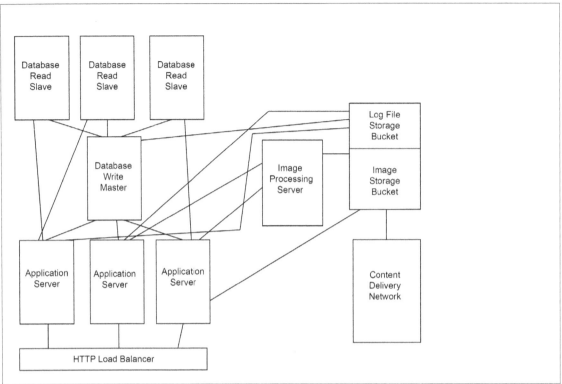

Figure 5-1 A cloud server backend showing the complexity involved in managing a large scale app backend.

Fortunately, in recent times, companies like Google have been offering **serverless** back end solutions, which allow web and native app programmers to write client side code in the language they know already and their app will be able to exchange data with a backend and they will never have to worry about administering the servers, scaling them, handling crashes, compressing and storing log files, creating backups, or installing software updates.

To get an idea of how serverless backends compare to their server counterparts, let's recall the list of application server tasks.

You'll see it's the same list from before but we've added in parenthesis the serverless solution to the problem:

- Authentication (Tokens)
- Authorization (Rules)
- File Storage (Static Storage Buckets)
- Validation (Rules)
- Data Sanitization (Automatic Output Filtering, NoSQL)
- Secure Operations (Functions)
- Hosting (Hosting)

Let's now take a look at each of these.

Tokens

Remember in the previous chapter we talked about the importance of authenticating users to prove their identities? We didn't explain it then, but application servers use cookies to accomplish this. Cookies are small pieces of data that include an ID placed by the server on the client after the initial request. They are subsequently sent back to the server by the client on any additional requests, thus allowing the server to identify the client. Firebase apps use tokens to authenticate users. What's the difference? Tokens liberate us from the need to have our data and authentication mechanism on the same server. They open the door for "Login with Google". This works to increase our app's user base by eliminating the difficulty in signing up for our app. The user can login using existing accounts on other popular sites. Of course, our app could also use Firebase's built in email/password login, which is simple as pie, but let's take a look at a third party login scheme as shown in Figure 5-2.

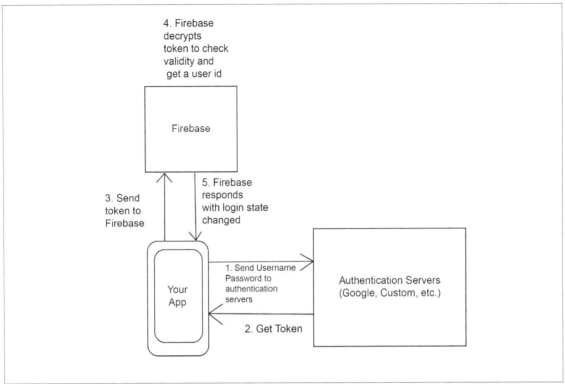

Figure 5-2 Third party token login flow. All subsequent data flows to and from Firebase and the authentication server essentially drops out of the flow.

The authentication server returns an encrypted token that the Firebase server can decode. When the server decodes it, it gets a user ID and any other data the authentication provider passes along in the token. **Tokens** work like a safe: you can put stuff in them, send them through the mail, and as long as the recipient has the combination, they can open the safe and get what's inside. This safe prevents malicious users from spoofing other users and stealing their data.

In a previous chapter we mentioned the difference between HTTP and HTTPS. It is very important that tokens, username, passwords, and anything else really, be sent over secure connections only. Fortunately, Firebase sets up the HTTPS connection automatically, so as long as our app only communicates with Firebase services using the code functions they provide, we're good to go! This is not automatic in the old architecture, or when using a custom authentication scheme. Setting up your own cloud server to use TLS requires special configuration.

Rules

The second half of authentication is authorization. Once we know the identity of the users, we need to make sure they have permission to do what they're trying to do. For example, if they are trying to delete a comment from the database, it had better be their comment to delete! This is where rules come in. Firebase has a rules syntax in JSON format, which you might recall from Chapter 3. This JSON doesn't get sent over the Internet though; rules are only in this syntax because developers are comfortable with it. The rules have two methods only: read and write. Write includes create, delete and update operations. You can specify different rules for updating and deleting by using the language constructors **data** and **newData**. The Firebase documentation does a great job explaining how the rules work. It can seem tricky at first, but expertise will come with practice.

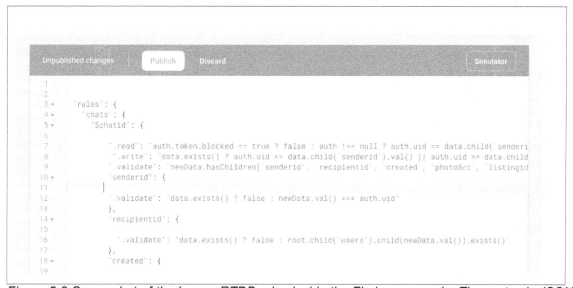

Figure 5-3 Screenshot of the legacy RTDB rules inside the Firebase console. The syntax is JSON, and each rule specifies which users can access each node, and what type and format of data is required. Any invalid data or unauthorized users will be denied. New apps should use Firestore (discussed later), but the rules operate in a similar manner.

In addition to authorization, the rules syntax has a method for validation. Validation rules make sure that each node of the database only accepts data that matches the format we expect (not too long, the right characters, etc). For example, you can specify that ages provided in the users node fall between 18 and 115. Or you can say that usernames contain between 3 and 25 characters and at least one special character.

The rules syntax replaces hundreds of lines of serverside code from an app written in the old architecture of the previous chapter. Be grateful for it. Figure 5-3 shows an example.\

Storage

Firebase uses Google Cloud buckets for storing user uploads (like pictures), just like the old architecture could (if the developer chose to). Storage has a separate rules syntax that controls who can upload or delete what and where. It works like the database rules syntax but has additional features added.

Security (Sanitization)

One of the biggest challenges of the old architecture was the difficulty in keeping the application and database servers secure. The instant we turn a computer into a server we introduce the possibility of hacking. Any additional functionality we add, like accessing a database or allowing user uploads, grows the **attack surface** and adds additional holes in our security that must be plugged carefully. The standard way to secure database servers is to filter input and escape output. In this way, our application servers act as a safety buffer between our database and our app.

Fortunately, with a serverless architecture, the NoSQL database eliminates SQL injection vulnerability. Also, cloud buckets are managed by people who probably know more about server security than the average client side developer. We still need validate contents our users upload with rules to prevent a security breach when our app users download them, but that is far easier than setting Linux file permissions properly.

It is, however, very important to learn the basics of security and not blindly trust the serverless backend to handle it all. Please check out the "Learning Security" section in Chapter 6.

Functions

As we learned in the previous chapter, some of the most important roles of the application servers were secure operations such as:

- Credit card processing
- Sending emails
- Sending notifications

Firebase handles these using Functions. Functions are written just like server programs in Node.js, but without the hassle of the server. You don't need to launch any instances or install or update or configure any software. You just write the functionality you need, in JavaScript, and upload it to Firebase using the command line tools in your Terminal or Command Prompt. Functions can be triggered by database changes, uploads to cloud storage buckets, authentication, manually with HTTP requests, and other ways.

As an example of a secure operation, let's look at processing credit cards. For reasons of legal compliance, your app likely won't handle credit card data, rather, you will use a third party credit card processing service called a payment gateway. Figure 5-4 shows the workflow for a payment gateway using a backend server function.

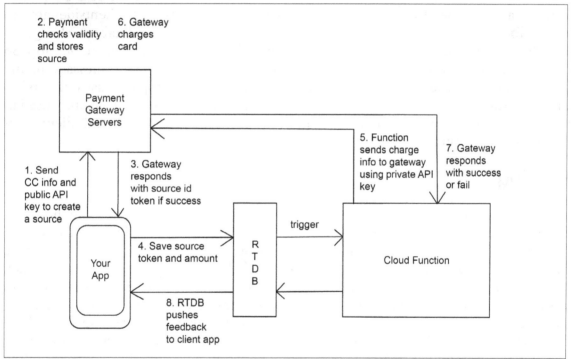

Figure 5-4 A payment gateway workflow. The user's credit card information is never sent to your backend functions. The gateway response in step 7 is sent to a URL you define in your functions as an HTTP trigger. This is also known as creating a **webhook**; and it works just like an API endpoint.

Other secure operations like push notifications work similarly, with your app backend functions contacting Apple or Google servers to actually send the notification.

Event Driven Real Time Database

So far, we have talked about how serverless backends replace application servers, but what about database servers? Serverless solutions do replace the need to host a database server. The Firebase real-time database (RTDB) has been replaced by Firebase Cloud

Firestore, and that is what your apps should use, but the RTDB still exists for existing apps. Firestore structures data differently than the RTDB, so storage and retrieval of data are a bit different, and the rules syntax is also different than the RTDB, but for our purposes right now it is still just an evented real-time database. Let's talk about what that means.

Unlike in the old cloud architecture from the previous chapter, Firebase will allow our JavaScript app to communicate directly with the database, rather than going through a serverside program to retrieve the data we ask for. The rules handle security rather than a serverside script. This eliminates the need for us to write serverside API endpoints. Instead, a real-time, two-way socket connection will allow our clientside app to **subscribe** to changes in data, thus, whenever the data in the database changes—regardless of who made the change—the server will push out the change to our app. So if we are chatting with Susie, and Susie's smartphone sends a new message to the database, the database will push (**publish**) that message to our app because our app has told Firebase that we want to subscribe to it. Publish / subscribe is a pattern often used in event driven programming—here to communicate between a server and client—but also in the client app code to respond to clicks, taps, swipes, etc.

Hosting

Just like application servers often hosted the web app too, Firebase can host our index.html, JavaScript and CSS. It works the same as the cloud based bucket storage for our user uploads, but with hosting we can associate a domain to our files. This means that we can buy a domain and **point** it to our index.html file in a Google cloud bucket. Pointing refers to specifying the IP address of the server hosting our file in the DNS record for our domain. By purchasing the domain, our chosen registrar gives us access to this record. As mentioned before, if we are building a native or hybrid app that will be downloaded from an app store, we don't need to host a website, but many apps have websites for promotional reasons. Also, many native mobile apps have corresponding web apps that access the same serverless backend.

New Architecture

So what do all these changes look like? Behind the scenes, Firebase no doubt employs load balancers and multiple application and database servers as shown in Figure 5-1, but you won't have to know about any of that. Your app will use Firebase as an intermediary to work with the database, storage buckets, and functions to work with anything else. Figure 5-5 illustrates the new architecture.

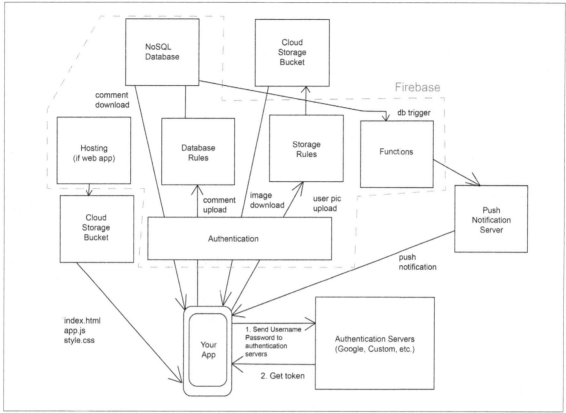

Figure 5-5 New backend architecture for a web app utilizing Firebase hosting.

The Firebase backend will respond the same to requests from native mobile apps or browser based web apps. The power of this architecture will not be apparent unless you try to build your own cloud based server backend. For now, just enjoy it.

The Firebase Console

Let's have a peak around the Firebase console. Even though you are a long way from being able to code an app, you actually know enough to grasp what goes on here.

1.   Open a web browser and go to https://firebase.google.com
2.   Create a new account and login.
3.   Create a new Firebase app.
4.   Go to the console.

On the left sidebar you can see, not surprisingly, the topics we just spent the entire chapter going over. Click around a bit to get familiar with the layout.

Review

I realize that this has probably felt like a whirlwind tour, but that's okay! When you start learning using the resources in the next chapter, you can refer back to this book anytime for a refresher. As you learn more about programming, data, and app development, the concepts in these first five chapters will solidify.

In this chapter we learned that a serverless backend allows our app to store and retrieve data like chat messages and photos without the need to launch and manage a bunch of cloud servers, regardless of how many users our app gets. We learned that serverless backends that implement functions can also handle payment gateways (for credit card processing), emails, push notifications and more. We then poked around the Firebase console to see how these features are implemented.

With this chapter complete, we have now covered nearly all of the background information you will need to begin learning to be a mobile developer. In the next chapter, we will look at the specific path forward—with web resources—that I recommend for you to learn programming and app development.

Chapter 4-5 Review

In Chapter 4 we learned that servers are just powerful computers connected to the Internet, but for reasons of performance, they are often dedicated to a single task. As app developers we usually only have to program the application servers, as email, authentication, and database servers are often controlled by a third party provider.

By looking at the common tasks associated with an application server, we got a glimpse of how complicated serverside programming can get. We learned what application servers do, and why they have to do so much. Application servers receive requests from client code and handle data (such as a username / password combination, or a comment, or a photo upload) and make sure the data is valid and that the user has permission to upload or download it. These requests are called API requests (API stands for Application Programming Interface). API requests are just plain old HTTP requests that follow a particular format specified by the designer of the API. Serverside programmers design their program to expect requests at a certain URL (called an API endpoint) and HTTP content format, and return the appropriate response (called API responses). Client apps that are designed to work with a particular API are said to **consume** the API. All of this terminology is extra knowledge that you will need only if your app interacts with third party APIs, as Firebase provides a code library that establishes those connections for us.

We learned that even though the cloud simplifies things considerably over buying and operating physical servers, developers of large scale apps still have to write a program that manages the servers themselves, which requires a more complete knowledge of server administration. In the days when this was required, app developers often had to be "devministrators", writing both app code and server management code.

In the not too distant past, building even a small scale app required learning client and server side programming, and a large scale app required learning client side, server side programming and server administration programming to manage a whole array of cloud servers and services.

Fortunately, those days are gone. In Chapter 5 we saw how serverless solutions from cloud providers allow app developers to learn a client-side language like JavaScript only, and still build a fully featured app with an array of backend servers. Firebase provided code will setup real-time, two-way socket connections with the clients that allow our app to exchange data without crafting network requests from scratch.

Chapter 6
Where Do I Go Now?

At this point, I sincerely hope that you have learned a lot and feel that you have acquired a basic knowledge of the technology stack on which mobile development depends. By now you should be able to explain what an app is and what an app does, as well as distinguish between native and web apps. You should also be able to explain what an app does not have to do, thanks to the environment in which the code runs. You should be able to look at existing mobile apps and recognize some of the common user interface features like navigation bars, menus, modal dialogs, and others. You should also be able to theorize how they might work, and know if they need a backend server, and if so, know what type of data gets stored and when that happens. You should also know the layout of the Firebase administrative dashboard, and be able to explain the purposes of the realtime database, authentication, storage, and functions, even if you can't use those tools yet.

You may feel like you still don't understand what you will have to do to build an app. That's okay! This book did not teach programming, but rather the background information required to begin programming.

Let's review this. As an app developer, you will likely not have to:

- Setup socket connections
- Launch, maintain, or manage cloud servers
- Know TCP/IP or much of HTTP
- Know how to convert the analog world into digital files or the physics of computer hardware

As an app developer, you will have to:

- Design a UI/UX
- Write code to keep your server and clients in sync
- Write code to keep track of the state of the UI
- Handle errors from inappropriate user actions (intentional or not)
- Handle errors from dropped connections or failure of third party software or open source code
- Write secure code
- Write code that interacts with APIs
- Program JavaScript serverside functions (even if you are a native developer)

Now it's time to look at how you will learn the nuts and bolts of app programming. This chapter functions as a detailed roadmap of learning HTML, CSS, JavaScript, Node.js, React, React Native and Firebase. It includes resources that I have found helpful. As mentioned in the Preface, this is by no means the only way to build a mobile application, but it is a way to get started. It is a path that, in my opinion, provides the most diverse skill set and allows for the most flexibility in its application. By learning web programming, you will be able to build web apps and mobile apps for iOS and Android. I recommend it because, as a self-taught developer myself, I truly believe in learning skills with a myriad of applications. Also, there is no reason that you cannot start on this path and break off and learn a different path later. Much of the core knowledge will serve you no matter what you end up programming. In addition, this path teaches you JavaScript, which is used as a serverside function programming language even if your client side apps are written in other languages.

This section recommends mostly websites. Books can be an effective way to learn the basics, but once you get to the point of learning frameworks like React, these frameworks change so frequently that books cannot keep up. Online documentation is intimidating at first, but the more you learn, the less this will be an issue.

Previously we defined web applications as applications hosted on a remote server and interpreted through a web browser. We're now going to define a web app as any application that uses JavaScript regardless of where it is stored or run. Using this definition, there are two types of web applications: **progressive web apps** (PWAs), and **hybrid web apps**.

Progressive Web Applications

Progressive web applications are available on the web (as opposed to downloaded through a store) but can access some of the native features of a smartphone. This approach has security concerns, and is dependent on the smartphone manufacturer allowing JavaScript code to access these features through an Application Programming Interface.

Progressive web applications use the underlying language structure as the web, that is, HTML, CSS and Javacript. Progressive web applications run in mobile web browsers but can be packaged with a **manifest file** and **cached** (i.e. downloaded into memory with a home screen icon that opens the web browser) on devices. They are not installed through the App Store or Google Play Store, and are thus a bit more unfamiliar to many users. The home screen icon functions like a browser bookmark, and special HTML 5 **meta tags** can tell the browser to hide the address bar (full screen mode), so that it looks more like a native app.

The advantage of progressive web apps is the ease of learning HTML/CSS/JavaScript versus native languages, and the fact that virtually every device (desktop, laptop, or smartphone) has a web browser.

The disadvantage of progressive web apps is that they don't feel like native apps. Users may not expect to download and cache an app from a website. HTML and CSS can mimic the graphic design of native apps, but do not always work out perfectly. Some things like push notifications work differently. PWAs are typically slower in performance and have some undesirable browser default behaviors, particularly on smartphones.

To learn more about PWAs, check out these links:

Google (https://developers.google.com/web/fundamentals/app-install-banners/)
Blog Post (https://medium.com/@applification/progressive-web-app-splash-screens-80340b45d210)
Mozilla Developer Network
(https://developer.mozilla.org/en-US/docs/Web/API/Service_Worker_API/Using_Service_Workers)

Hybrid Web Applications

As a result of the shortcomings of progressive web applications, people developed hybrid applications, that is, applications that are programmed in JavaScript but use premade bits of native code to allow them to be packaged and sold on the App Store and Google Play Store. Hybrid web applications combine the features of both native and progressive web applications. Once downloaded and installed, hybrid web applications are indistinguishable from native applications.

Hybrid apps have the look and feel of native apps, nearly all of the functionality of native apps (with modules), but allow the core functionality to be coded in JavaScript. They have been around awhile and are used by some big companies. Different types exist, and they work differently internally but the end result is the same, a JavaScript application that runs on a phone.

Hybrid apps have access to native components and usability. This, as you will discover in your learning, aids in UX (user experience) design greatly. In addition, people are used to installing apps through the App Store, they're used to native apps asking for permission and having a native view of app permissions on one screen. Even if a progressive web app has the capabilities you need, there's a lot to be said for having your app work as expected by the user.

The chief advantage of hybrid apps over native apps is that they combine the run anywhere nature of JavaScript with the user experience and functionality of native apps. You can write JavaScript and create a progressive web app and—with some substantial changes of code—use a packager to install your app on both iPhone and Android platforms.

The disadvantage of hybrid apps is that—depending on your choice of framework— your app may depend on third party modules to access all of the smartphone features. Sometimes these "shims" work great, other times the path could use some ironing. Sometimes getting a lot of third party code to play together produces troubles.

One of the best hybrid app frameworks is called React Native*. Although the code used for the web application and a React Native app won't be identical, it is all JavaScript, which sure beats having to learn three different languages and two different operating systems! We will summarize the distinctions between the types next.

*According to the React Native website, a React Native app is not considered a "hybrid" app. This depends on how you define "hybrid" app. If you say a hybrid app is one that uses a browser container embedded in native code, then no, a React Native app is not a hybrid. This book uses a more general definition that a hybrid app is one that is programmed in JavaScript. As is true of everything in computers, opinions differ and tempers run high. This book uses the general definition of hybrid app and thus considers those apps to be hybrid. This is because "native app written in JavaScript" isn't as catchy as "hybrid", and this technical distinction is more confusing to beginning learners. Once you finish this book and understand the basics, feel free to use any terminology you prefer. At this point, do not let these semantics confuse or discourage you.

Summary of Mobile App Types

I hope the previous discussion on the types of mobile applications did not discourage you. The distinctions between them are a bit technical and difficult to explain without prerequisite knowledge, but charting that roadmap is what this book is all about. Fortunately, you won't have to choose a path until after you finish this book. Figure 6-1 summarizes the differences in the three types of mobile applications. There are other ways to build a hybrid app too, some that use HTML/CSS, but this book focuses on React Native.

Type	Native Apps	Hybrid Apps	Progressive Web Apps
Languages Used	Device Specific	Javascript and JSX	HTML, CSS and Javascript
Host	Smartphones	Smartphones	Web
Installed Via	App Store or Google Play Store	App Store or Google Play Store	Not installed, but can be downloaded and cached
Functionality	Full	Full with modules	Limited, based on browser / device
Environment	Operating System	Operating System + React Native Container	Web Browser

Figure 6-1 Comparison of native applications, hybrid web applications, and progressive web applications.

Figure 6-2 shows the topics required to learn to build progressive web apps. This book recommends learning PWAs, and then optionally learning hybrid apps using React Native.

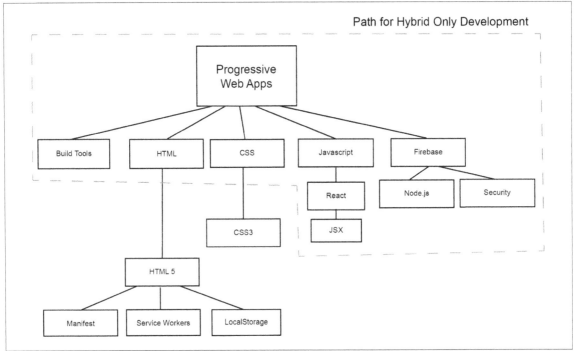

Figure 6-2. Topics required to learn to build PWAs. Learning to build progressive web apps is a great primer for learning to build hybrid apps. If you are only interested in hybrid apps, just focus on the topics inside the dashed lines.

With that said, I will not sugar coat it, the road ahead of you is long and will be exhausting at times. Stick with it!

Learning HTML

Learning HTML is pretty straightforward. Like any markup language, it's just a matter of memorizing a few tags. For mobile programming with React Native, you won't use HTML, but you will use JSX, and it works the same. To take the path recommended in this book, I would recommend buying an introductory HTML/CSS book, or just reading online to learn about the basic tags, attributes, ids, and classes. Those are the only concepts you need to know to use JSX later on. Even if you learn using the web based interactive courses, a book on HTML/CSS is a handy reference.

If you are interested in programming progressive web apps as an alternative to native or hybrid apps, you can learn more about the meaning of the confusing looking header that begins each HTML document (the DOCTYPE, the meta tags) and also about HTML 5.

HTML 5 added new tags and a whole bunch of new APIs that browsers implement to allow your JavaScript programs to become full featured progressive applications. That is why some books are dedicated specifically to HTML 5, although learning the old and new HTML separately is not necessary, as the new stuff is not difficult. Most books on HTML also address CSS—at least to a beginning level—since they are like coffee and cream.

Resources for learning HTML:

Any HTML book (it's easy to learn)
Codecademy (https://www.codecademy.com/learn/learn-html)
Khan Academy (https://khanacademy.org)
Udacity (https://www.udacity.com)
W3 Schools (https://www.w3schools.com)

Learning CSS

Even though CSS is written in plain English, it can be a dickens to master. Historically, all the different browsers interpreted CSS code differently, but it has begun to standardize. You will see some books that specifically cover only CSS 3, while other books focus on "the basics" of CSS 2. CSS 3 includes graphical improvements that make the web easier on the eyes, and books focused on it alone are usually targeted toward developers who already know CSS.

As mentioned in the HTML section, if you are planning on writing hybrid apps using React Native, don't bother becoming a CSS expert. React Native uses styling commands similar but not exactly the same as CSS, so spending hundreds of hours learning the CSS specification inside and out will not help you.

A closely related topic to CSS is Responsive Web Design (RWD). RWD focuses on using CSS to create layouts that tailor automatically to the screen size. This allows you to develop user interfaces that look good on laptops, tablets and smartphones.

As an aside, you may encounter the acronyms LESS and SASS during your CSS study. They are mini programming languages with functions and variables designed to make it easier to write mega size CSS files. They're neat if you write thousands of lines of CSS for progressive applications. If you want to learn one, learn SASS. SASS files need to be transpiled into regular CSS before a browser can read them. LESS and SASS are for progressive web apps only, as React Native organizes big style sheets using different techniques.

As mentioned previously, the same resources used to learn HTML can be used to learn CSS. After learning the basics, purchasing books or reading blog posts specific to RWD may be helpful too. React Native uses a syntax for layouts similar to CSS 3 Flexbox, a common RWD tool that any RWD book will introduce.

Once you know the basics you may also find it useful to read the specifications themselves. These are not particularly friendly introductions, but they are the direct source of the information.

Resources for learning CSS:

Learning CSS (https://www.w3.org/Style/Examples/011/firstcss)
CSS2.1 Specification (https://www.w3.org/TR/CSS21/)
CSS Specifications Reference (https://www.w3.org/Style/CSS/specs.en.html)

Learning JavaScript

Enough pretense already! We are finally here. It is time to learn programming for real! There a number of ways to do it and the best is based on what kind of learner you are. Even if you used books to learn HTML/CSS, I recommend web based interactive courses for learning JavaScript. These will allow you to practice coding (and see the results) as you learn, which helps tremendously. Only once you have mastered the basics and really want to get an in depth understanding of the language do I recommend buying books.

ECMAScript is the standard on which JavaScript is based. Unfortunately, the syntax changes constantly as features are added. New features are great, but it can make it daunting for new programmers. It's a bummer that after spending so much effort learning JavaScript it changes on you, but that's the reality. The new functionality is not mandatory, but nearly all of the documentation of React and React Native will make use of some features of this syntax.

Resources for learning JavaScript:

Codecademy (https://www.codecademy.com/)
Khan Academy (https://khanacademy.org)
Udacity (https://www.udacity.com)
W3 Schools (https://www.w3schools.com)
Mozilla Developer Network (https://developer.mozilla.org)

Learning React

Eventually you will build a real app with real complexity. When this happens you will find it is almost unmanageable without some organization to your code. Frameworks, written by others, can help organize your code into manageable chunks. How the code is classified and chunked depends on the framework chosen.

It is possible to learn multiple frameworks; it is also possible to combine frameworks to some extent. Two possible paths to take are React with or without Flux, or a Model View Controller framework. There are too many MVC frameworks to bother mentioning. If you would like to learn more about them just do a web search.

Using an MVC framework you break your code into models, views and controllers. The models are in-memory representations of your database data. The views are HTML/CSS templates that are populated with model data. Often a templating language is used to avoid having to write one from scratch. The controllers **bind** the models to the views with the Pub/Sub pattern described earlier in this book, that is, when the model data changes (perhaps from a Firebase update), the model triggers an event which the controller subscribes to, and repopulates the view with the new data. You often include a **state machine** to keep track of the app state, which is just a controller that initializes or removes controllers as applicable. Once you become a proficient programmer you can explore MVC frameworks or even create your own.

React (https://reactjs.org) is a framework for PWAs that does things differently. The criticism of the MVC/State Machine method is that it emphasizes "separation of languages" over "separation of concerns". React mixes the views right into the components, and each component keeps track of it's own state. There is no need to learn a templating language, as React uses JSX, which looks and works almost exactly like HTML. React does not require your entire application to use it, you can mix it with any code you have already, even an MVC framework. React alone handles the views, or the UI, and does not make any assumptions about how you move data from the server into memory. The data can be stored in components' state variables, or in models, or the data can be stored in a Flux pattern. Learning and implementing Flux (https://facebook.github.io/flux/docs/in-depth-overview.html) is not necessary to use React, but it makes the framework more complete. Many libraries that implement Flux are available; one popular library is called Redux (https://redux.js.org/basics/usagewithreact).

You can see that React is one piece of one path toward a web app or a JavaScript based mobile app. React is a great way to structure web applications, but I think React really shines when used with React Native, which is the next step.

Resources for learning React:

The React website (https://reactjs.org/tutorial/tutorial.html)

Learning React Native

Once you have built a PWA or two with React, you are almost ready to put your app on a real mobile device! You may also find that PWAs are sufficient for your app needs, and in that case you're done! If not, the final bridge is called React Native (https://facebook.github.io/react-native/); it helps minimize the amount of multi-language programming we have to do to have a web, iOS and Android app. There are alternatives to React Native: other packagers, some that use a browser container, are often combined with MVC frameworks, that can be installed on smartphones. You are free to explore those on your own.

Figure 6-3 shows the topics required to learn hybrid web apps once you know how to build progressive web apps using React. Now however, we are further dividing the hybrid mobile apps into distinct tracks using different frameworks.

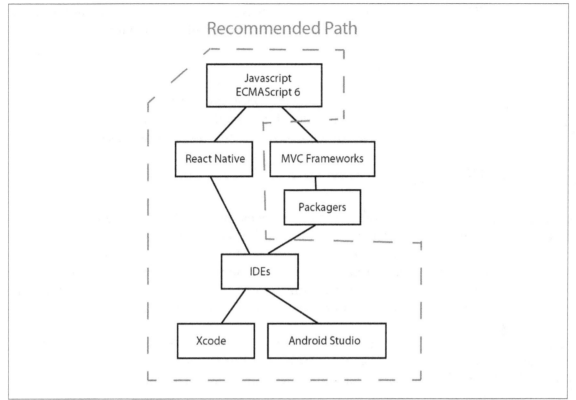

Figure 6-3 The topics required to learn hybrid web applications. The route recommended is in dashed lines.

React Native consists of just enough Objective C, Swift, or Java code to translate your JavaScript app into an installable native app. You will be able to work with all of the native views and features provided by the iOS or Android platforms, although some may require third party modules or modules you write yourself.

The learning curve here requires getting used to the new environment, Xcode or Android Studio, using native views, React Native's take on CSS, ECMAScript6 syntax and some new error messages. The online tutorials are a great way to get up to speed fast. These tutorials show how to test the app on your own device, as well as get it onto other people's devices, and then eventually into a store.

The hardest part about learning React Native is that you are becoming a native developer whether you like it or not. Some errors will occur in native code, and are debugged through the native IDE. See Chapter 7. The native developer documentation is written for native programmers, which makes it challenging for JS programmers. JavaScript errors can be debugged through a Chrome plugin. The workflow for building a React Native iOS app involves the Terminal, Chrome, and Xcode. It may help to buy a book on the native IDE and read through enough to get comfortable with it.

Resources for Learning React Native:

The React Native Website (https://facebook.github.io/react-native/)
Apple Developer Documentation (https://developer.apple.com/documentation/)
Android Developer Documentation (https://developer.android.com/docs/)

Learning Firebase

As mentioned in Chapter 5, if your app needs a backend, serverless is the way to go, and Firebase is a great choice. Firebase Firestore is the database to learn and use (not the legacy RTDB). Firebase operates as a serverless backend for both PWAs and hybrid or native apps. Fortunately, the online Firebase documentation is some of the best I have encountered anywhere in the programming world. Some features, like storage, will require working with the Google Cloud, which has its own documentation.

There are guides to get started, YouTube videos and full API documentation. Using Firebase with React Native is easy, blog posts can teach you how, and there is already code on GitHub to shim the gap even more if you don't want to write that code yourself.

Resources for Learning Firebase:

Firebase Getting Started Guide (https://firebase.google.com/docs/web/setup)
Firebase Cloud Functions Examples (https://github.com/firebase/functions-samples)
React Native with Firebase Blog Post (https://firebase.googleblog.com/2016/01/the-beginners-guide-to-react-native-and_84.html)

Learning Node.js

Node.js (https://nodejs.org) is server software that allows us to write serverside programs in JavaScript. As mentioned before, because of Firebase Functions, we won't actually have to create any server instances, but instead will drop our code right into the Firebase backend. Although you will already know JavaScript by the time you reach this point, you will need to learn some specific things about Node. Fortunately, by the time you get here, learning from online documentation will not be so daunting.

Learning Security

Security is an extremely important part of learning to program. I have not found a single comprehensive resource to address security from the perspective of a front-end / serverless mobile and web developer. However, there are some general security principles that you should be aware of, and simple web searches can yield all the information you need on them. The following are applicable to any programming language, in any environment:

- Implementing the least privilege principle
- Implementing defence-in-depth
- Filter input, escape output
- Be mindful when user input changes environments
- Utilize encryption tools (HTTPS, hashing, signatures, etc.)
- Use strong passwords
- Don't store passwords or API keys in version control
- Create an organization security policy
- Keep software up-to-date
- Keep current on security threats
- Exercise good physical security

The **least privilege principle** simply means granting only privileges that are needed. In your Firebase rules, for example, if your users don't need the right to read from a specific node then don't grant that write.

Defence-in-depth refers to making sure that each level of your program has safeguards to limit the damage of an attack. It is essentially applying the least privilege principle over and over. If you write a function that grabs a list of email addresses from your database, for example, and it loops through to email all of them, it would be wise to include a limit on the number of iterations of that loop. Your database rules should make sure that only valid email addresses make it into your database, but the max iterations in your function code acts as a catch to limit the spam sent out if someone succeeded in injecting extra email addresses into the database.

Many, if not most, security vulnerabilities arise whenever data changes environments, such as when database data is displayed in a browser, or when user input is put into a database, or when user data is taken from a database and used to create an email. An example of these vulnerabilities is illustrated in Figure 6-4. In all of these scenarios, if the programmer simply assumes that the data is secure and takes no measures to filter the input, a vulnerability will exist. This is why filtering input is so important. You can also escape output, which means using escape characters to prevent the data from being interpreted as code in it's new environment. Escaping output occurs naturally from Firebase, and most templating languages have it built in automatically.

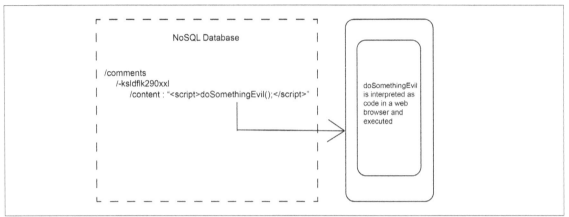

Figure 6-4 Vulnerabilities are often created when code changes environments. App developers need to be sensitive to those changes. Here we see a Cross-Site-Scripting attack by putting JavaScript code inside HTML tags that are displayed by a mobile browser. The browser assumes the tags are part of the app and executes the code. Escaping output prevents this kind of attack.

The mathematics of encryption are complex, and not necessary for the developer to know. However, you do need to know how TLS and HTTPS protect your users and yourself from man-in-the-middle attacks and wire sniffers. It may be helpful to read up on the basics of **symmetric** and **asymmetric encryption**, **hashes** and **digital signatures**, as these techniques are commonly employed by third-party APIs.

Next, good passwords go a long way. Change them from time to time, and enable two factor authentication on the Google account you use for Firebase and the Google Cloud. If you don't already, learn to use a passphrase to generate strong passwords. This means, take a phrase that you know and use all the time, like "All Good Bar B Que Uses Steak Sauce" and take the first letters of each word to create AGBBQUSS.

If working in a developer team, it's a good idea to craft a security policy, a written statement of how your organization will protect passwords and enforce your rules, and it can specify at what layers of your app each security tactic happens. For example, you could say that all data will be displayed in the browser through a templating language.

In addition to these basics, you should be aware, and know steps to prevent, the following specific attacks:

- Cross site scripting (**XSS**)
- Cross site request forgery (**CSRF**)
- Man-in-the-middle attacks
- HTTP header and form spoofing
- Query injection
- Email header injection
- Denial Of Service / Distributed Denial of Service

You will need to seek out full explanations of these yourself, however, web searching will yield volumes of information. It is always a good idea to have as much knowledge of potential security threats, even if they are technically not applicable to your environment.

As for serverside security, we touched on it briefly in the chapters on servers and serverless backends. As mentioned there, going serverless increases your app security a lot, but there are still some topics you will need to learn. Before you write serverside functions for your app you should at least be familiar with the threats, even if they won't affect your particular app. Firebase eliminates some of the threats but not all of them. Fortunately, most of these threats are very well known and easily prevented with proper input validation.

Resources for learning security:

As mentioned, there is no one resource I have found that addresses complete security from a client side programmer's perspective. Try doing individual web searches for the topics listed in this section. Once you have acquired the skills to understand them, you might check out books on serverside language security (PHP, Linux). Also check out the resources below for more information.

OWASP (https://www.owasp.org/index.php/Category:Attack)
Google (https://developers.google.com/web/fundamentals/security/)
Mozilla Developer Network (https://developer.mozilla.org/en-US/docs/Web/Security)

Learning APIs

APIs are extremely useful to programmers as they allow our apps to leverage third party functionality. However, learning how to write code that interacts with an API can be like learning a small programming language. You have to read the documentation thoroughly to understand which endpoint to access, how to structure your request, and how to process the response (including error handling). See the Appendix for tips on how to read API documentation.

To use many APIs, you may need to have your app authenticate itself. The exact flow of this depends on what you are trying to do, but it can be as simple as including a public API key in the src attribute value of a script tag. This is how you could use Google Maps (https://developers.google.com/maps/documentation/JavaScript/tutorial) in your web app for example.

Sending emails, payment gateway interactions, and push notifications are all API interactions that will happen in your serverside functions. These functions will require private API keys (unlike the aforementioned public keys), which you will want to store as constants in your Firebase hosting rather than hard coding into your index.js file (to avoid accidentally pushing them to version control). These constants are easily set with the Firebase command line tools.

Review

In this chapter we reviewed in detail the differences and similarities between progressive and hybrid apps. We looked at the steps required and some recommended resources for learning progressive mobile development, and saw how many of these steps will help learn hybrid and even native development to an extent also.

You can always go to the specifications directly for the purest information. Just like in Chapter 3 when we talked about the importance of protocols in computer networking, every computer language has to have a very detailed specification in order to be implemented properly by all the different manufacturers. These specifications are freely available and, though not the easiest way to learn something the first time, provide the most precise and accurate information on a particular technology or language. Computer science majors and the authors of books tend to get their information directly from the specifications. Even image files and language features like tokens have specifications.

Chapter 7
What Tools Do I Need?

This chapter will present and explain some of the tools you will need as a programmer, regardless of whether you program web or native mobile apps. I have tried to keep the explanations here applicable to both web and native development to the extent possible, but there is a clear bias toward web / React Native development.

Computer (required)

Many mobile programmers use Apple computers because of the requirement to use Xcode to package your apps for the App Store. Web programmers also like them because Mac OS X is built on UNIX, and that gives them a built-in Terminal app, which works well with Linux boxes and their software with no additional configuration. Android development can be done on Windows or Mac OS X, so anyway you slice it, an Apple computer gives you the most versatility.

Xcode and Android Studio (required)

If you are programming native apps, or when it comes time to package your React Native app into an installable mobile app, you will need Xcode and / or Android Studio. Xcode only runs on Apple computers. You will learn the bare minimum about using these programs in React Native tutorials, although there is a lot more information on the web and in other books. Unfortunately, a lot of the help and documentation is written for native languages, which can be difficult for JavaScript programmers to understand. It might be smart to buy a book on Xcode and read just enough to get comfortable with the programming environment.

Both Xcode and Android Studio fall in the category of **Integrated Development Environments** (IDEs) which are programs that typically combine a plain text editor, a debugger and linter, unit testing software, dependency management code and a compiler. They do all this for their native languages only. To get this functionality in JavaScript for web or React Native apps, a whole suite of individual programs is required. Figure 7-1 illustrates this. Don't worry, we will talk about each of these programs next.

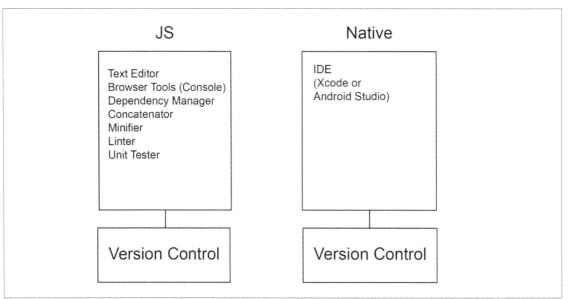

*Figure 7-1 Native app IDEs versus individual programs in a typical JavaScript workflow. Both workflows utilize version control (also known as **source code management**).*

Text Editor (required)

You need a plain text editor to write and save code. Note that this differs from a word processor, which saves files in it's own format for creating documents. Plain text is just that, plain old text—typically computer code. Picking the best plain text editor is a controversial topic among programmers, I'm just going to recommend Sublime Text 3 (https://www.sublimetext.com) without justification. You are welcome to explore others on your own and you will likely discover other recommendations in other books throughout your journey. Although IDEs for native development languages contain plain text editors, I recommend having a standalone editor for editing code in other languages. Note that TextEdit, which is installed by default on Mac OS X, is a plain text editor but may require some configuration in the preferences to get it to work as expected. See Figure 7-2. Notepad is also a plain text editor on Windows.

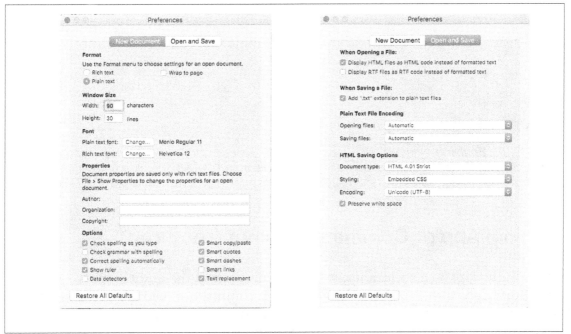

Figure 7-2 Setting preferences in TextEdit. Format should be plain text and display HTML files as code should be checked.

Browser Developer Tools (required)

Web browsers include developer tools that allow you to see a lot of useful information about the web code in a web app. The developer tools also contain a console which functions as a JavaScript debugger. The process to enable the developer tools differs from browser to browser. In Firefox, it is under Tools->Web Developer, and then select any of the options. In Safari, go to Develop->Show Web Inspector. In Chrome, select View->Developer. If you have any trouble finding the tools (perhaps you have a different version of these browsers) just do a web search to find the instructions to turn them on.

With the developer tools on, you can highlight elements of the HTML and see the CSS styles that the browser applied to them. You can even edit them right there by double clicking on any property, to see how different styles change the look.

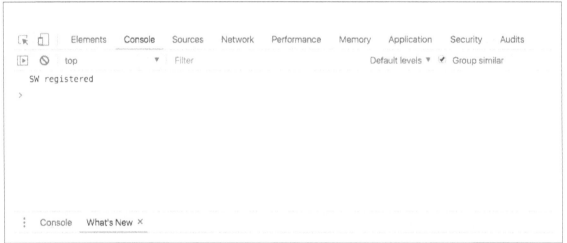

Figure 7-3 Enabling developer tools gives access to the whole source code (HTML/CSS/JavaScript) of the site, as well as a console for JS debugging, and other tools. A plugin even allows for React specific debugging. The debugger can even be used for React Native applications.

Terminal App or Command Prompt (required)

You won't get very far into JavaScript books before one of the authors will recommend getting some code from NPM. You don't need the command line to download and install Node.js (the program that includes npm), but to use npm to install software, you will need to use the command line. You will also use the command line to upload your Firebase functions to the serverless backend.

On Apple computers use the Terminal app in Applications/Utilities. On Windows use the command prompt. More about NPM and its uses is in the Appendix.

Version Control (optional)

Version control is a solution to a problem you have likely encountered at some point in your life. If you have ever worked on a document from multiple places, perhaps at work and at home, or have collaborated on a document with multiple people, you have probably realized that passing around thumb drives and emailing it is not a great workflow.

Version control allows all computers and collaborators to hack on the same **codebase** (programmer speak for all the files in your application folder) without losing track of each other's changes. Even though your first projects as a coder will be extremely simple—often single file apps—I believe it is important to start using version control from day one.

There are many choices for version control, but I recommend Git (https://git-scm.com), because the website GitHub (https://github.com) has a huge library of open source code for all sorts of problems, and because Git offers a seriously friendly app called GitHub Desktop (https://desktop.github.com/). No command line skill is required. Just get an account, download the app, and start a new repository (which is just your application folder). When you change the files in this folder and save them, Github Desktop will show you the changes you made to the files. When you're ready, click commit to commit the changes to your codebase and click Sync to push them up to your server. You should always remember to hit Sync before you start hacking away to make sure you have incorporated the latest changes. If you try to sync an older version up to the cloud, and the new changes conflict with it, Github Desktop will throw an error and tell you to sort it out.

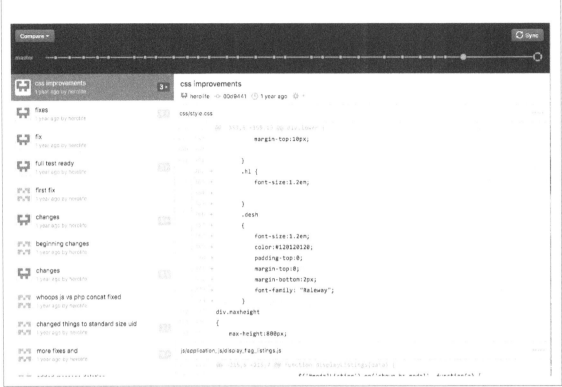

Figure 7-4 Using GitHub Desktop. It shows a timeline of all commits (code changes you made and added to the repository) and also the code itself.

A Local Server For Testing (optional)

To test your JavaScript code you need only drop it into an .html file and open it in a web browser. But on occasion you will encounter code that for security or other reasons will not run from the file:// protocol, which is the protocol you get when you simply double click on an .html file and it opens in your web browser (HTML 5 **Geolocation** is one example). In this case you can either run the code on Firebase hosting, or test the code by turning your computer into a temporary local server. The Firebase command line tools have a serve command to do this. See this link for more information (https://firebase.google.com/docs/web/setup#run_a_local_web_server_for_development).

Build Tools (required)

Heads up: this section contains some advanced material that may not make any sense until you encounter it in other books. Keep it handy as a reference.

Just like mobile apps are built on a large stack of technologies, software is often built out of other software. As your JavaScript programs build in complexity, you will find that they have a large stack of dependencies, either open source code or code that you have written before. Including all of these files when they are needed can be a chore. Unfortunately, there are so many ways of solving the problem it can get even more confusing than the problem itself. I will attempt to sort out some of the confusion here.

I have lumped all of these tools together under the category of build tools, although some of them are not technically used at build time but rather run time. I have taken some liberty with the terminology here, for the sake of simplicity and explaining how these work. The tools fall into the following types, with the workflow shown next.

- Pre-build module installers- npm (https://www.npmjs.com), yarn (https://yarnpkg.com)
- Build time module loaders- browserify (https://browserify.org)
- Transpilers- babel (https://babeljs.io)
- Concatenators (cat, Linux command line tool)
- Minifiers- uglify (https://github.com/mishoo/UglifyJS)
- Linters- eslint (https://eslint.org)
- Testers- jest (https://jestjs.io/en/)
- Task runners- manual shell script (to automate above tasks)
- Local testing server
- File watchers (https://facebook.github.io/watchman/)

Each of these tools has multiple examples, the ones shown above are just single examples and I don't endorse them, feel free to look for others. There are also all-in-one solutions that combine the tools above with a nice GUI, so that they become a sort of JavaScript IDE. You can look those up too, if you like. Choosing a workflow involves familiarizing yourself with each of the tools, what they do, and then picking the ones you like best, while avoiding tools that duplicate what was done already.

All of these tools are designed to make coding monster size JS apps more manageable, unfortunately, they are difficult to understand for newbies. Without encountering the problems of monster size apps, the reasons for such complexity are not clear. Furthermore, to computer science majors and pro programmers coming from other languages the needs for these tools are second nature, so they often skip the explanation.

Technically, you can avoid the complexity of using dependency managers by simply downloading and linking the files to your index.html file yourself, but as your code grows, this method is not practical. Open source code versions change constantly, and if you include the wrong version your code may not work.

NPM is a way that JavaScript programmers distribute open source code. It is a **dependency manager**, meaning it will automatically install the necessary dependencies you specify into a node_modules file. If your code does not require any node modules (which it won't unless your app uses an open source framework like React or requires serverless functions) then you won't need to use npm. However, if you plan to deploy your code onto Firebase hosting, you will use npm to install the necessary command line tools and create the app folder to upload your app to their servers.

Once your app open source code dependencies have been installed by npm into a node_modules folder, you code up your app. You won't be packaging and distributing your app components publically through npm, but you will definitely want to be able to write the code for the components in separate files, and utilize ES6 syntax for all of it's benefits. Coding in separate files is awesome for organization, but it's difficult to keep track of which files require which other files, and including the same file twice throws errors. A better way is to use a module loader, which will allow you to load your files just like node modules. This is where require statements come in. A module loader will translate the require statements and include the files properly for you.

If you use any ECMAScript6 or later syntax, your code will have to be **transpiled** (think "translated into old JavaScript") for older JavaScript **engines**.

Ok, we have all of the code we need in our folder and it is readable by a browser, but is it really practical to distribute our code this way? Think of all the HTTP requests a browser would have to make to load the app this way. Not it's time for **concatenation** and **minification**. Concatenation puts all our JS code into a single file, minification cuts out all whitespace and comments and reduces variables to the minimum size possible. This workflow is shown in Figure 7-5.

Linters are utility programs that scan your code for errors or possible errors that could lead to problems down the road. They also make syntax suggestions much like a word processor makes grammar suggestions.

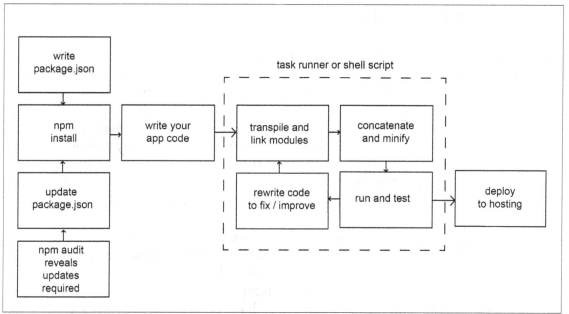

Figure 7-5 Common JavaScript workflow. The part surrounded by dashed lines is the build process and is typically automated (with the exception of trying out the code yourself). This workflow applies to progressive web apps using React. React Native apps will use some of the same tools, but will compile in the native IDE.

You will often see unit testing mentioned in JavaScript books. Unit testing is a method of programming where the programmer develops tests alongside the development of each component, and then runs those tests every time a new component is added to the larger application. This method helps discover bugs long before they cause problems, and is essential to the development workflows of large apps built by large teams. For a self-taught, solo developer, unit testing will do nothing but slow you down. You can safely ignore this subject when it comes up in advanced JavaScript books, unless you plan on going on to be a professional programmer.

Task runners are programs that run a bunch of tasks automatically, to eliminate typing individual commands. Some task runners have GUIs for easier use. Of course, a shell script, run on the command line, can replace the need for these.

Resources for learning build tools:

Blog Post (https://www.slant.co/topics/1488/versus/~npm-browserify_vs_yarn_vs_bower)
Blog Post (http://stackoverflow.com/questions/35062852/npm-vs-bower-vs-browserify-vs-gulp-vs-grunt-vs-webpack)

Pattern Library (optional)

As you learn to program, you will develop apps for fun according to instructions you read in books and online. Often times, when you begin to develop something on your own you will ask, "I know I did that before, but how did I do it?" Implementing my own pattern library saved me hours of rewriting user interface code that I had developed for other projects. A pattern library works like a journal of your code; when you develop a cool component for an app, whether a responsive navbar, a photo carousel or whatever, you gather up the HTML, CSS and JavaScript that makes it work and drop it into an HTML file, along with some explanatory documentation. That forms your pattern library. It looks great and you can access it forever, whenever you need it.

When I first encountered the idea of a pattern library, it occurred to me that the same concept could be used for pure JavaScript snippets of commonly used functionality. It's also a great way to document your progress as a coder. I even use it to store links to GitHub projects I've used in the past. Many templates for creating your own pattern library exist on GitHub, and big companies also have released pattern libraries you can use as examples.

More Tips

As a developer you don't need to reinvent things. Unless you are very design oriented, creating a beautiful interface with HTML and CSS or even native views can be difficult. If developing a PWA, Bootstrap (https://getbootstrap.com) can be very helpful. They also have themes for purchase, including some with common web application functionality. These will help you prototype your idea quickly. There are also similar themes by others for native views.

Then there is an endless amount of open source code available on GitHub, but pay attention to the licenses (not all open source licenses are the same). It is also tough to find good code on GitHub because of the shear amount of it. This is where staying connected through blogs and conferences helps immensely.

Congratulations

You made it through this book! I have no doubt that a lot of the concepts introduced here are still quite hazy, particularly in regard to computer networking, serverless functions, and what exactly your application code will have to do. Do not fear! This book was merely a top level overview of those topics and perfect understanding was not expected. As brief as this book was, it contained a considerable amount of the knowledge you will need as a mobile app developer. Remember, mobile apps written in JavaScript are high up in the technology stack: your app will work with data as strings and files—not binary numbers—and the necessary conversions to binary data will be provided by the many, many layers of code underneath it. As you work through the path defined in Chapter 6, I assume you will return to this book to refresh your memory of where certain concepts fit into the larger stack. I hope this book continues to serve as a roadmap as you battle on. Few are brave enough to tackle mobile app development without classes or an instructor—and make no mistake, it will be difficult—but you can do it! I sincerely hope you are able to build the next big thing! Good luck!

APPENDIX
Miscellaneous Topics and Tips

This Appendix includes exposition of some miscellaneous topics that I struggled with during my self-study of programming. It is not contiguous with the previous chapters and will require learning the material in the roadmap laid out in Chapter 6 before it will be helpful.

Open Source Code

Open source code refers to programs that programmers have released for use by other programmers. One common source of open source code is GitHub. Open source programs are named such as you have full access to the uncompiled source code (as opposed to commercial apps where you only buy an executable file and the assets).

They are always released with a license. Some common licenses are listed below:

- Creative Commons (https://creativecommons.org/licenses/)
- General Public License (https://www.gnu.org/licenses/gpl-3.0.en.html)
- MIT License (https://opensource.org/licenses/MIT)

Depending on the license the program may be free for all use (commercial and private), or free for private but available for purchase commercially. It's important to read the license especially if you are a building an app you plan to use commercially.

The disadvantages of open source code include difficulty of use (due to poorly written or inadequately detailed README files), and possible lack of maintenance or stability issues. If the code doesn't work, you have no one to call. Forums and IRC chat are your only fallbacks.

Security with open source code is a double-edged sword. Vulnerabilities in open source code do pop up from time to time, sometimes with widespread consequences. The open source nature makes it easy for hackers to discover vulnerabilities. On the other hand, the open source nature of it means that a lot of good people can examine the source for bugs or malicious code as well, and eliminate them before they get pushed out.

GitHub

Sometimes learning how to use someone else's repository is difficult, especially as a self-taught developer. Professional repos often employ directory structures that are second nature to professional programmers but cryptic to everyone else. Some insight can be gained by learning the build tools that create the directory structures. Part of the reason I suggested learning a bit of Linux in Chapter 4 was to familiarize you with package managers and the folders of files they use. Programmers often use similar directory structures with similar folder names. The more you know about programming, the less you will be thrown by confusing folder names like "source", "build" and "bin".

Programmers do not tend to like writing and it often shows in help files and README files. When viewing a GitHub page, new programmers often wonder how to get the functionality into their app. There is no single answer. Sometimes you go to a GitHub page to copy and paste some code from the example files. Other times you go to see an example, and watch it work. Advanced developers go to clone a repository and hack on it, possibly to contribute their changes it back to the project. Most often as a new developer, you will simply visit the page to copy and paste from the example code, or to install the package into your app. If you are copying code, you find the file you want and view the code right in GitHub's web editor. If you are installing the package, the README file should contain the instructions. Typically, it will list the npm command to install the project locally into your app folder.

When looking a GitHub project and trying to figure out how to use it, you should ask the following questions:

- Am I looking for an example or am I trying to install this in my app?
- How do I install this?
- What global variables does this package expose?
- What are the interface properties and methods of those globals and how are they used?

The first question is up to you. The other questions should be answered by the README file. Open source code is typically written as a module, which is a standard way of packaging code so that it can work as plug and play with other code. Your code works with it through some functions known as an interface. An interface is just like the knobs on an oven. You use the functions to do things without needing to know how the code works, just like the knobs on an oven allow you to set temperature and cook time without needing to know how the oven works, or knowing how to build an oven yourself. A brand new oven will drop right into your kitchen with little modification (plug and play). Code modules utilize this same concept. When installed, you will access the functionality by putting a require statement at the top of your app code. A JavaScript module loader will interpret that as part of your build process (see Chapter 7). Your app code will then be able to use the module functionality through the variable that you named in the require statement. That variable will likely be an object with methods (functions) that form the interface.

If GitHub is a place for open source code and just directs you to NPM to install the project you may wonder what the difference between NPM and GitHub is. GitHub is a source for open source software in all languages. The website hosts code repositories that allow people from all over the world to collaborate on open source code. It also hosts GitHub pages that typically contain example code demonstrating the use of the package, and in-depth READMEs. NPM, on the other hand, is a command line based dependency manager and a package distribution source with that handles the installation of open source code and all of its dependencies. The NPM website has some limited documentation on the packages, but this is largely barebones information about the versions and installation and is generally not comparable to GitHub pages.

NPM

As mentioned before, NPM (https://www.npmjs.com) is a package manager for JavaScript code. It is run on the command line. but it also has a companion website that contains documentation on how to use it and documentation on the individual packages. To be an effective JavaScript programmer, you will need to be able to install open source code into your app folder. Open source code nearly always depends on a whole lot of other open source code, and NPM will handle installing dependencies and checking version compatibility for you. You will also package your PWA for Firebase hosting and functions as an NPM package, even though you won't be distributing your app publically through NPM. Packaging your app this way allows NPM to audit your dependencies for version incompatibilities and updates.

There are only a few basic command line skills you need to use NPM. First, you must understand the concept of a present working directory. This is the directory you are in on the command line. Most often you will work from the root folder of your app (your app folder), as opposed to subdirectories your app may have such as images, css, or js. You must also understand the format of command line commands, as mentioned in the previous section.

The following are a handful of tasks you will likely use:

- npm install (to install all packages in package.json)
- npm install some_package (to install a package)
- npm –v (to check the version of npm you have installed)
- npm audit (to scan all your packages in node_modules for issues)
- npm update (to update all your packages)
- npm start (to start some executable defined in the folder)

There are two ways to install packages locally into your app folder. The first is to run npm install some_package. You replace "some_package" with the name of the package you want to install. The second way is to write the package name and version number in a plain text file you save format as JSON and save as package.json in your app folder, then running npm install with no arguments will install every package in package.json. To view the possible version numbers of a package, visit npmjs.com and search for the package and view the version history. You generally want the latest stable version (not a development version), unless software dependencies force you to choose an earlier version.

Linux Basics

Often programming books just present you a command and say "type this in!" without any background information. Authors assume that everyone reading their book knows the Terminal and also how to use it. Not only must you open a Terminal on Mac OS X, but there are a couple things that are absolutely critical to know before you can get started. The first is the present working directory (the folder you are in on the command line). When you first open the Terminal on Mac OS X, it will be your home directory.

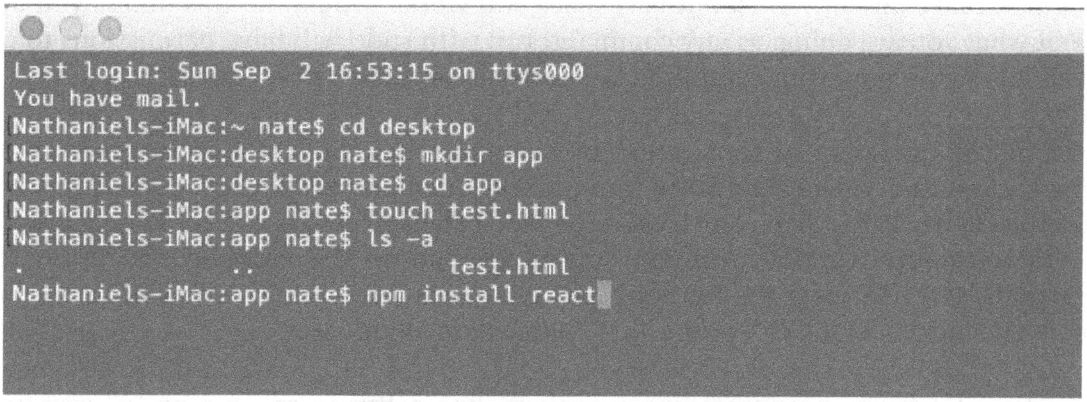

Figure A-1 The terminal app on Mac OS X is a UNIX style command line. This screenshot shows some common commands typed in at the shell prompt. At the end of each line, pressing Enter tells the computer to execute the command. Here we change directories from the user home directory to the user desktop, create a new directory called app, change to it, create a file named test.html, list all the files in the pwd, and then type in the command to use npm to locally install some code into our app folder.

The next concept is the shell prompt. That is the dollar sign at the end of terminal prompt. The shell takes commands when you type them in and press Enter. You can make a new directory called newapp (mkdir newapp) and press Enter, and change to it (cd newapp) and press Enter. When you type in a Linux command, it is generally executed in the context of the present working directory, unless you throw a flag to indicate otherwise. Linux commands usually take the following form:

$ Executable Function –Flags Arguments

Example:
$ npm install –g firebase-tools

The commands listed as bullet points in the NPM section previously should look less confusing now. NPM is the executable (command line program), install is the function (what you want npm to do), '-g' is a flag for the command, and 'firebase-tools' is an argument (an optional parameter that tells the install function what to do). The only way to know what commands and flags are available for a certain executable is to look at the documentation for that package. The same is true for the functions of a certain executable and the arguments those functions expect.

Sometimes you will run commands requiring you to temporarily get root privileges with the superuser do command **sudo**. This requires you to type your password at the prompt. The prompt won't show what you type in, you just have to go on blind faith that you didn't make any mistakes, but backspace still works. Do not do this unless you are sure of what you are doing, as any command run with sudo will have permissions to do just about anything on your computer. Seek advice carefully before proceeding.

Linux, like all operating systems, works by having a whole bunch of processes running in the background, called **daemons** (pronounced "demons"). These processes are what make the OS work. Just like your JavaScript code listens to events like clicks and swipes, the OS constantly working to update the image the on the monitor, and listen for commands, etc. To view the working processes use ps –aux. This is similar to the Activity Monitor in Mac OS X or the Task Manager in Windows.

It can be a bit frightening installing command line software and typing "y" granting permissions you don't fully understand! It is important to stick to the beaten paths of computer programming and only use software recommended by reputable brands or people. I would say don't do anything that makes you uncomfortable, but then you probably wouldn't do any programming at all! You will have to step outside your comfort zone, but do research on programs in books and forums before you go granting permissions to shady command line utilities. It is also a bit unnerving when you trust the software you're installing but you get a few dozen virtually unintelligible warnings! Fear not, that's common with "bleeding edge" software, if anything doesn't work, search the errors you got in your search engine of choice.

Trouble Learning JavaScript

I won't lie, learning JavaScript was difficult for me. Some of the difficulties are as follows:

- JavaScript has a long and troubled history that often makes the reason behind it's idiosyncrasies unclear
- Different browsers implement it differently
- Programmers like OOD, but the classless nature of the core language before ES6 led to the development of a myriad of class libraries
- JavaScript is constantly evolving: ES6, etc...
- A lack of a standard IDE makes the build process, as detailed in Chapter 7, a complex mess of individual programs and homemade scripts
- JavaScript has multiple environments leading to different code: Core, Client Side, Node
- If you are learning JavaScript as your first language you will be learning programming, OOP/D, event-driven / asynchronous programming all at the same time
- Authors of JavaScript books and blog posts use dozens of libraries and frameworks often with little explanation to how they work or why they came to be (background knowledge is assumed)

So with all these obstacles, what shall we do? Often, when you deal with programming books and online docs, you will have questions that are not answered. Are all these warnings a problem? What if I typed this in wrong? How do I undo this? Remember search the error and use Stack Overflow (https://stackoverflow.com) as necessary.

Object Oriented Programming

Early in my study of web development I encountered posts that said "everything in JavaScript is an object". I then saw others that claimed "JavaScript is not object oriented". I was so confused I didn't know what to think. I now know the logic behind these two sentences but I also know they are not true. First of all, it is imprecise to speak of a language as object oriented or not object oriented. Every programmer immediately knows what is meant by that usage, but this language can be very confusing to beginners. Object orientation is a design principle that encourages the programmer to write programs composed of individual reusable components. That's it. An "object-oriented language" is just a programming language that implements features that make coding in this way easier. These features are **classes**, **inheritance**, **interfaces**, **type hinting**, and others. You can write procedural code in a so-called object oriented language, although some languages force a object oriented structure on you more than others. You can also write reusable components in a completely procedural language. A more precise sentence would be: JavaScript, before ES6, did not implement many features of **Object Oriented Design** (OOD), but did and does have a data type of object.

Object Oriented Design (a.k.a. Object Oriented Programming) is a way of designing and writing programs so they work more like mechanical objects. Some of the most widely used patterns that form the basis of this type of design are the Factory Pattern, Pub/Sub and the Singleton Pattern. You can spend as much time as you like studying OOD, but in a single sentence, OOD seeks the same goal as the often used acronym DRY (Don't Repeat Yourself). It is not necessary that you study the OOP books in depth. It would be good to learn the basic principles of **composition** and **inheritance**, as it will help you design components in React, and using React and other third party code will virtually force you to program in an OO way, so you will be learning it at the same time.

The purpose of OOD is organization, but also reusability. To make things reusable they have to be general. In other words, it makes more sense to build a dishwasher than a soup spoon washer. Building reusable code modules that can serve uses outside your app is the process of **abstraction**.

When you first learn OOD, it may seem like it's all just putting extra code in between things, like adapters for Apple computers. With the factory pattern, data mappers, or the database abstraction layer, this is largely true. These patterns are like code components that pick the right adapter based on what is needed. But when you change something down the road, it will be simple. Don't feel pressured to introduce a massive amount of abstraction in your early programs. Every program will balance getting the job done and planning for future growth and code reuse. Don't worry if the reasons for some of the more advanced OOD features are not apparent right away. Always remember, OOP is not different code, it's just a different way of organizing your code that makes it easier to change later, avoids duplication of code, and makes it easier to discover bugs, especially when using objects that someone else wrote. With **type hinting**, **abstract properties** and **methods**, and **unit testing**, you can more easily ensure that your code is functioning as it should before deployment, but none of these features are required to build a JavaScript application.

Asynchronous Programming

Code, both OO and procedural, runs from start to finish. In OOD, calling code will utilize methods in classes that are often defined in other files, but make no mistake, the code still runs from start to finish. Asynchronous code, is event based, so it runs chunks of code only when certain things happen (mouse clicks, data received from a remote server, etc.) As a JavaScript programmer, much of the code you write will be async code. Async code is not different code from OO or procedural; 'async' just refers to the function callbacks or promise block that wrap the code. The code inside the callback or promise blocks will be procedural and / or OO.

Fortunately, JavaScript now has a Promise syntax which makes async coding almost effortless. All your Firebase calls will return promises that can be chained together. Simply follow example code in the docs or on GitHub and you won't have any problems. Unfortunately, a lot of documentation about Promises and their theory is rather esoteric and long-winded. Using Promises does not require a college degree, but coding async incorrectly can lead to problems like undefined variables, race conditions, variable clobbering, scope issues, attaching events to stuff that doesn't exist yet, etc, so studying a bit of the theory is important.

In Firebase functions, your functions may execute on different cloud servers than the RTDB or Storage, so any interactions with the RTDB or Storage will return promises, because of the latency between the function call and the action on the remote server.

The Reason For Models and Local Storage

Suppose we get data from the server. We could immediately render that data to the **Document Object Model** (DOM) as HTML, but what if we later wanted to change that data not only on our screen but on the server (like updating our username, for example)? We would have to use DOM access to get it again and then change it and send it to the server.

Or what if we wanted to open up a modal window with the full data? We would have grab all the data from the DOM, get each text node content, and then redisplay it into a modal template (or make a second trip the server for the same data). What about loading the data into memory and using it when we need it? This is a model. A model is an in-memory representation of data. But what happens if we refresh the browser window? Our models are gone! Which is what we want, but what if we want to have some data **persist** when the mobile app is not connected to the Internet and only update if it goes stale (the same data on the server has changed without our client updating)? Local Storage allows us to do this, and forms the basis of progressive web apps.

JSON is the language of models and the method of transfer from server to client and vice versa. When our Firebase callbacks receive data, we simply assign that data to a model, which if we are using an MVC library might mean actually "creating" a model. If we are using React, it's really just a matter of copying the snapshot to this.state. As app data gets passed to and from many React components, it eventually makes sense to have a separate component that handles all the data. For more advanced data handling check out Flux (https://facebook.github.io/flux/docs/overview.html).

Reading API Documentation

In order to build complex functionality into your apps you will likely want to leverage third party APIs, so that you don't need to reinvent things. Back in the day, APIs were simply serverside endpoints, and access required you to craft networking requests such as AJAX requests in a very specific format, and parse the response you got with a JSON or XML parser. Some APIs still operate like this, but most provide a library of client side code to access them. This means that instead of coding up network requests you will simply make a function call. These libraries are often distributed on GitHub.

Firebase is a perfect example of this. We will only interact with Firebase through the global variable defined in their code. This global variable (typically an object) has methods (functions) which we will call. These functions may take other objects defined by their API as arguments, and will return other objects defined by their API. Learning to read the API documentation is thus a critical skill of a web developer, but can be tricky.

Don't be scared by abstract terms like **static** and **interface**. If you want to know what those mean, check an OOD textbook. Instead, try to visualize the whole API as nested objects of objects with methods. Figure A-2 shows a fictional API called CookieOvenAPI. It defines a single global object, with all other objects **namespaced** behind it. The global has one method called bake(), that takes a string representing the type of cookie to be baked as an argument. The global also has a property called Cookie, which itself is an object. Behind the scenes, using code unknown to us, bake() returns a Promise, which means it promises to either give a us a cookie or an error. In the case of of an error, we get a Error object—also defined by the API. In the case of a successful bake, it returns a Cookie object that has an array property called ingredients, and a method called eat() that takes no arguments and returns null (nothing).

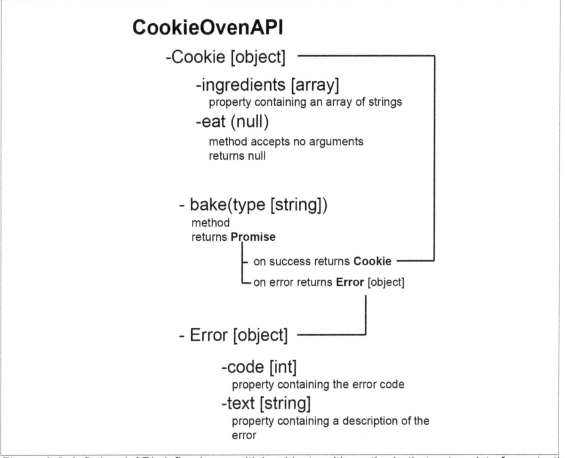

Figure A-2 A fictional API defined as multiple objects with methods that act as interfaces to the objects. Creating a sketch like this as you read the API docs can be helpful.

Let's say we install this code with npm, and require the global in our code and assign it to a variable called cookieMaker, the code to eat a chocolate chip cookie might look like this:

```
var cookieMaker = require('CookieOvenAPI');
cookieMaker.bake('chocolate_chip').then(cookie => {
        cookie.eat();
}).catch(error => {
        console.log(error.text);
});
```

When reading API documentation, try to visualize the code in action. HTML is actually the perfect method of displaying API docs with the use of hyperlinks, but HTML does not provide a physical view of these relationships in action. Sketching a map like Figure A-2 can help you visualize the connections between different aspects of the API and thus write code that works properly.